Enoch Arden and Other Poems

U

U   ®

The Riverside Literature Series

ENOCH ARDEN AND OTHER POEMS

BY

ALFRED, LORD TENNYSON

WITH BIOGRAPHICAL SKETCH AND
EXPLANATORY NOTES

The Riverside Press

CONTENTS

U.

BIOGRAPHICAL SKETCH.

ALFRED TENNYSON was the third of twelve children of the Rev. George Clayton Tennyson, LL.D., rector of the village of Somersby, in Lincolnshire, and was born on August 6, 1809. So apart from the world was Somersby that even the news of Waterloo did not reach it for some time after the great victory was won. The low fen country of England in which the village lies has indeed such a quiet beauty of its own that it seems the very home of peace. Such surroundings were as well adapted as any could have been for the development of a nature like Tennyson's. Thackeray's daughter, Mrs. Ritchie, has given the most suggestive glimpses of the poet's childhood. She tells of him as a sturdy boy of five, opening his arms to the wind, letting himself be blown along by it, and as he went, making his first line of poetry, "I hear a voice that 's speaking in the wind."

Another story of Mrs. Ritchie's must be told, as showing how a family of young people who nearly all were to do something one day in poetry entertained themselves : "These handsome children had, beyond most children, that wondrous toy at their command which some people call imagination. The boys played great games like Arthur's knights ; they were champions and warriors defending a stone heap, or again they would set up opposing camps with a king in the midst of

all sat

his history underneath the potato bowl, — long, end-
less histories, chapter after chapter, diffuse, absorbing,
unending as are the stories of real life of which each
sunrise opens on a new part: some of these romances
were in letters, like 'Clarissa Harlowe.' Alfred used
to tell a story which lasted for months, and which was
called ' The Old Horse.' "

There are anecdotes, too, of Tennyson's early
attempts at writing, which, under the stimulus of a
sympathetic household, were not few. While he and
his brother Charles were still mere boys they determined to face the world with a little book of verses.
A firm of booksellers in Louth was persuaded to pay
ten pounds for the copyright of the small volume
which in 1827 appeared under the title " Poems by
Two Brothers." As in most juvenile verses it was
easy to see how greatly the young poets' minds bore
the impress of their studies and reading.

There was nevertheless no lack of individuality in
Alfred's mind, if not yet in his work. The fresh im-
pulse of university life was needed to bring forth the
best in the young man. A little schooling and his
father's instruction had prepared him by 1828 to enter
Trinity College, Cambridge. It was in large measure
through his friendships that Alfred Tennyson's development at the University came about. He soon found
himself one of a group of undergraduates known as
' The Apostles," a literary society which bound together the choicest young spirits of the University.
Of all " The Apostles," Arthur Hallam, the son of the
historian of the Middle Ages, seems to have been en-
dowed with the rarest gifts of mind and spirit. In
Tennyson's enthusiasm for his friend he was said to
be."

Another of their coterie said : " His was such a lovely nature that life seemed to have nothing more to teach him." So closely allied were the two young men by every sympathy of taste and feeling that their friendship soon grew to be a very part of their lives.

Upon his father's death in 1831, Tennyson left the University without taking his degree. Meanwhile, in 1830, Hallam and he had together made an expedition to Spain — not unlike Byron's to Greece — with the purpose of helping the rebellion against the tyranny of Ferdinand. They carried with them money and letters written in invisible ink, and altogether bore themselves like true conspirators.

Through the college terms and the vacations spent mainly in Hallam's company, Tennyson's chief concern had been poetry. His "Timbuctoo" was honored as the Chancellor's Prize Poem in its year, and even attracted the notice of the public press. It was in 1830 that he brought forth the volume which set up his first public claim to be considered a poet. Its title was " Poems, chiefly Lyrical," and in its contents are to be found poems which still appear in Tennyson's collected works. The critics reviewed the volume with moderate praise, and one of them had the strange foresight to write, with special reference to " The Poet : " " If our estimate of Mr. Tennyson be correct, he too is a poet, and many years hence may he read his juvenile description of that character with the proud consciousness that it has become the description and history of his own work." The faith his friends had in him is shown by Hallam's prophetic words one day in the garden of Somersby rectory. " Fifty years hence, people will be making pilgrimages to this place."

Todd

next volume, a little larger than the previous book and containing some of the poems which still hold a high place amongst his best of their kind. " The Lady of Shalott," the first pledge of his devotion to the Arthurian legends, was one of them.

In 1833 came the crushing news of the death of Arthur Hallam, now doubly dear as the betrothed lover of Tennyson's sister. Travelling for his feeble health in Austria with his father, he was seized with an intermittent fever, and died in Vienna. The bereavement at once drove Tennyson — from his earliest days given to solitude and introspection — more than ever before into himself. For nearly ten years after Hallam's death, the poet published practically nothing, and held himself much aloof from men, leading — except for sojourns in the country with family and friends — a rather lonely, busy life in London. In this period it is said that most of " In Memoriam " was written, though it was not published till 1850. Besides linking inseparably the names of Tennyson and Hallam, this wonderful poem is for all men who mourn the loss of a friend the expression of the complete progress of grief, from its first stunning blow, through its gradual stages, to the final mastery of resignation.

In these outwardly silent years of its production it is believed that Tennyson, busy with much poetic work beside, was consciously perfecting the gifts in which, with the certainty of genius, he had ample confidence. The time, however, was not wholly without its friendships and pleasures. To an extract from one of Carlyle's letters to Emerson we are indebted for a graphic picture of the Tennyson of this period : " One of tl   hock of rough dusty-dark hair; bright, laughing hazel eyes; massive aquiline face, most massive, yet most delicate; of sallow-brown complexion, almost Indian-looking; clothes cynically loose, free-and-easy; smokes infinite tobacco. His voice is musical metallic — fit for loud laughter and piercing wail, and all that may lie between; speech and speculation free and plenteous: I do not meet, in these late decades, such company over a pipe'"

In 1842 appeared in two volumes the "Poems" which determined Tennyson's position as an English poet of the first rank. Previously he had been known but to the few. Now his careful matured work of ten years was instantly recognized as individual and high. New editions of the book were speedily called for, and in 1845 Tennyson's name was put upon the pension list for an annuity of £200. From this time forward the poet's fame was secure. In 1847 "The Princess" was given to the world, and met with immediate popularity. But it is the year 1850 which stands forth as the most important in the poet's career. His marriage with Miss Emily Sellwood, a niece of Sir John Franklin, the Arctic explorer, then took place. Twickenham, already associated with poetry through the name of Pope, became their first home. Earlier, in the same year, Tennyson published, at first anonymously, "In Memoriam." Scarcely had it appeared when Wordsworth died, and the laureateship became vacant. The warrant creating Tennyson Poet Laureate was dated November 19, 1850; on March 6, 1851, he was formally installed. It is interesting to read that at his first appearance at court, he wore the court dress of the aged poet, Samuel Rogers, that Words-worth and that each poet arrayed himself in it at Rogers's house before the ceremony.

It was not long before another of his most characteristic works was completed and brought forth, for the book to which "Maud" gave the title appeared in 1855. We have seen how, as early as 1832, the Arthurian legends were occupying the poet's mind. In 1859, he published the first four of the "Idylls of the King." As we have them now they were not completed for some years, several being added in 1869, — including the "Morte d'Arthur," incorporated from the volume of 1842, — and the last in 1872.

The Idylls give evidence of one of the most distinguishing marks of Tennyson's genius, — his devotion to his native land. As became the Poet Laureate, he spoke constantly from a strong national feeling. "Maud" was in large measure his outcry against the materialism which he felt as a menace to his nation. "The Charge of the Light Brigade" shows clearly enough how his countrymen's noble deeds could move him. "The War" with its ringing refrain,

"Form! form! Riflemen form!"

gives an instance of his power to awaken others. The volume of 1864, taking its title from "Enoch Arden," and containing such poems as "Sea Dreams," displayed another side of his English sympathies.

His own life the while was the ideal life of a poet, touching humanity through its friendships, yet almost always remote from the crowd. Leaving Twickenham, he went to live at Farringford, near Freshwater in the Isle of Wight. The climate of Farringford was not found always congenial with Mr.   became too much an object of curiosity to strangers. It was thought best, therefore, to live, at least for a part of the year, elsewhere, and by 1867 the Tennyson family was established at the retired estate of Aldworth, near Haslemere in Surrey. Between this place and Farringford the time thenceforth was divided. The oldest son, Hallam, as years went by, became his father's constant companion. The only other child, a son, Lionel, died in 1886, at the age of thirty-two, having begun a promising diplomatic career.

After the appearance of the last of the Arthurian poems in 1872, Tennyson entered upon a period of dramatic production, but in spite of the poetic beauty of many passages in Tennyson's plays, it cannot be said that they have given him a rank amongst English dramatists at all corresponding with his place amongst the poets. First of the dramas, "Queen Mary" was published in 1875, and a year later Mr. Henry Irving brought it out in a condensed form at the Lyceum Theatre in London. "Harold," in 1877, was the next play, and has never yet been acted. Other plays followed at intervals up to 1884, when "Becket" was published. Since then Mr. Irving has produced it successfully.

"Ballads and Other Poems," published in 1886, brought together many of the stirring shorter pieces written during the same years with most of the plays. In the year of "Becket's" publication, Tennyson was gazetted Baron of Aldworth and Farringford. As he had gained popularity in 1865 by declining a baronetcy, so in certain quarters he lost it for a time by the acceptance of a peerage. The elevation caused no abatement of his work, for in 1885 "Tiresias," a volume,

in the next year, one of the unsuccessful plays, "The
Promise of May," gave the title to another new book.
In 1889 was published "Demeter and Other Poems."

Of necessity the end was now drawing near. Yet
as late as the spring of 1892, his semi-dramatic pas-
toral poem had its first production in New York, and
was greatly liked. In the summer of 1892 he was
busy with the proofs of a new volume, "Akbar's
Dream," but he did not live to see its publication.
Early on Thursday morning, October 6, after a short
illness, he died at Aldworth. His bed was by the
window, through which a flood of moonlight fell upon
him. It was a scene for the poet's own pen to describe.

It is impossible to sum up in the brief space that remains a complete estimate of the essence of Tennyson's
poetic greatness. In any analysis of it, the purity,
elevation, and depth of thought, the pervading quality
of imagination, and the constant beauty of structure
must primarily be reckoned with. In other words, his
mind was amply adequate to supplying him with the
most noble and lovely themes, and his mastery over
his art enabled him to put them into noble and lovely
forms. He gathered up in himself many of the beauties of poets who went before him, and has won the
tribute of so much imitation — often by persons no
doubt unconscious of imitating — that nearly the
whole body of English poetry in our second half cen
tury has been different because of him.

NOTE   It should be said that most of the biographical material fo
this sketch has been drawn from Arthur Waugh's *Alfred Lord
Tennyson A Study of his Life and Work.*

U,

ENOCH ARDEN.

LONG lines of cliff breaking have left a chasm;
And in the chasm are foam and yellow sands;
Beyond, red roofs about a narrow wharf
In cluster; then a moulder'd church; and higher
5 A long street climbs to one tall-tower'd mill;
And high in heaven behind it a gray down
With Danish barrows; and a hazelwood,
By autumn nutters haunted, flourishes
Green in a cuplike hollow of the down.

10   Here on this beach a hundred years ago,
Three children of three houses, Annie Lee,
The prettiest little damsel in the port,
And Philip Ray, the miller's only son,
And Enoch Arden, a rough sailor's lad
15 Made orphan by a winter shipwreck, play'd

Enoch Arden appeared as the principal poem of the volume
bearing its name in 1864 It is the main product of a period
of reaction from the work which dealt, in the *Idylls of the
King*, with the great legends of England. As in other poems
of its period, Tennyson attempted to draw near to the actual
life of the English people. The sympathetic reader will feel
especially in the poem the fitness of the means to the end in
view; the many metaphors of the sea, the stress that is laid
upon the elements of superstition and the supernatural, — elements well in keeping with the characters of the story. The
beauty of the descriptive passages needs no pointing out

7 **Danish barrows** burial mounds supposed to date from the
Danish in

Among the waste and lumber of the shore,
Hard coils of cordage, swarthy fishing-nets,
Anchors of rusty fluke, and boats updrawn;
And built their castles of dissolving sand
20 To watch them overflow'd, or following up
And flying the white breaker, daily left
The little footprint daily wash'd away.

A narrow cave ran in beneath the cliff;
In this the children play'd at keeping house.
25 Enoch was host one day, Philip the next,
While Annie still was mistress; but at times
Enoch would hold possession for a week:
"This is my house and this my little wife."
"Mine too," said Philip, "turn and turn about:"
30 When, if they quarrell'd, Enoch stronger made
Was master: then would Philip, his blue eyes
All flooded with the helpless wrath of tears,
Shriek out, "I hate you, Enoch," and at this
The little wife would weep for company,
35 And pray them not to quarrel for her sake,
And say she would be little wife to both.

But when the dawn of rosy childhood past,
And the new warmth of life's ascending sun
Was felt by either, either fixt his heart
40 On that one girl: and Enoch spoke his love,
But Philip loved in silence: and the girl
Seem'd kinder unto Philip than to him;
But she loved Enoch: tho' she knew it not,
And would if ask'd deny it. Enoch set
45 A purpose evermore before his eyes,

36 A line which skillfully foreshadows the tragedy of the
poem.

To hoard all savings to the uttermost,
To purchase his own boat, and make a home
For Annie : and so prosper'd that at last
A luckier or a bolder fisherman,
50 A carefuller in peril, did not breathe
For leagues along that breaker-beaten coast
Than Enoch. Likewise had he served a year
On board a merchantman, and made himself
Full sailor ; and he thrice had pluck'd a life
55 From the dread sweep of the down-streaming seas :
And all men look'd upon him favorably :
And ere he touch'd his one-and-twentieth May
He purchased his own boat, and made a home
For Annie, neat and nestlike, halfway up
60 The narrow street that clamber'd toward the mill.

Then, on a golden autumn eventide,
The younger people making holiday,
With bag and sack and basket, great and small,
Went nutting to the hazels. Philip stay'd
65 (His father lying sick and needing him)
An hour behind, but as he climb'd the hill,
Just where the prone edge of the wood began
To feather toward the hollow, saw the pair,
Enoch and Annie, sitting hand-in-hand.
70 His large gray eyes and weather-beaten face
All-kindled by a still and sacred fire,
That burn'd as on an altar. Philip look'd.
And in their eyes and faces read his doom ;
Then, as their faces drew together, groan'd,
75 And slipt aside, and like a wounded life
Crept down into the hollows of the wood :

51. Fu
67 *S.*

There, while the rest were loud in merrymaking,
Had his dark hour unseen, and rose and past
Bearing a lifelong hunger in his heart.

80 So these were wed, and merrily rang the bells,
And merrily ran the years, seven happy years,
Seven happy years of health and competence,
And mutual love and honorable toil;
With children; first a daughter. In him woke,
85 With his first babe's first cry, the noble wish
To save all earnings to the uttermost,
And give his child a better bringing-up
Than his had been, or hers; a wish renew'd,
When two years after came a boy to be
90 The rosy idol of her solitudes,
While Enoch was abroad on wrathful seas,
Or often journeying landward: for in truth
Enoch's white horse, and Enoch's ocean-spoil
In ocean-smelling osier, and his face,
95 Rough-redden'd with a thousand winter gales,
Not only to the market-cross were known,
But in the leafy lanes behind the down,
Far as the portal-warding lion-whelp
And peacock-yewtree of the lonely Hall,
100 Whose Friday fare was Enoch's ministering.

Then came a change, as all things human change.
Ten miles to northward of the narrow port

91. Osier basket.

96 Many English villages have an old stone cross in the market-place.

98. The heraldic device over the portal to the hall, supposed to stand as a guard (warding).

99 A yew-tree cut after the fashion of old gardening, into the f

Open'd a larger haven: thither used
Enoch at times to go by land or sea ;
105 And once when there, and clambering on a mast
In harbor, by mischance he slipt and fell:
A limb was broken when they lifted him :
And while he lay recovering there, his wife
Bore him another son, a sickly one :
110 Another hand crept too across his trade
Taking her bread and theirs : and on him fell,
Altho' a grave and staid God-fearing man,
Yet lying thus inactive, doubt and gloom.
He seem'd, as in a nightmare of the night,
115 To see his children leading evermore
Low miserable lives of hand-to-mouth,
And her he loved, a beggar: then he pray'd
"Save them from this, whatever comes to me."
And while he pray'd, the master of that ship
120 Enoch had served in, hearing his mischance,
Came, for he knew the man and valued him,
Reporting of his vessel China-bound,
And wanting yet a boatswain. Would he go?
There yet were many weeks before she sail'd,
125 Sail'd from this port. Would Enoch have the
        place?
And Enoch all at once assented to it,
Rejoicing at that answer to his prayer.

    So now that shadow of mischance appear'd
No graver than as when some little cloud
130 Cuts off the fiery highway of the sun,
And isles a light in the offing · yet the wife —
When he was gone -- the children — what to do?

131. At   .   . .   .
light staid

Then Enoch lay long-pondering on his plans;
To sell the boat — and yet he loved her well —
125 How many a rough sea had he weather'd in her!
He knew her, as a horseman knows his horse —
And yet to sell her — then with what she brought
Buy goods and stores — set Annie forth in trade
With all that seamen needed or their wives —
130 So might she keep the house while he was gone.
Should he not trade himself out yonder? go
This voyage more than once? yea, twice or thrice —
As oft as needed — last, returning rich,
Become the master of a larger craft,
135 With fuller profits lead an easier life,
Have all his pretty young ones educated,
And pass his days in peace among his own.

Thus Enoch in his heart determined all:
Then moving homeward came on Annie pale,
150 Nursing the sickly babe, her latest-born.
Forward she started with a happy cry,
And laid the feeble infant in his arms:
Whom Enoch took, and handled all his limbs,
Appraised his weight and fondled father-like,
155 But had no heart to break his purposes
To Annie, till the morrow, when he spoke.

Then first since Enoch's golden ring had girt
Her finger, Annie fought against his will:
Yet not with brawling opposition she,
160 But manifold entreaties, many a tear,
Many a sad kiss by day by night renew'd
(Sure that all evil would come out of it)

142 **Voyage** must be read as a dissyllable, not too pro-

Besought him, supplicating, if he cared
For her or his dear children, not to go
155 He not for his own self caring but her,
Her and her children, let her plead in vain ;
So grieving held his will, and bore it thro'.

For Enoch parted with his old sea-friend,
Bought Annie goods and stores, and set his hand
1.. To fit their little streetward sitting-room
With shelf and corner for the goods and stores.
So all day long till Enoch's last at home,
Shaking their pretty cabin, hammer and axe,
Auger and saw, while Annie seem'd to hear
1.. Her own death-scaffold raising, shrill'd and rang.
Till this was ended, and his careful hand, —
The space was narrow, — having order'd all
Almost as neat and close as Nature packs
Her blossom or her seedling, paused : and he,
1.. Who needs would work for Annie to the last,
Ascending tired, heavily slept till morn.

And Enoch faced this morning of farewell
Brightly and boldly. All his Annie's fears,
Save as his Annie's, were a laughter to him.
1.. Yet Enoch as a brave God-fearing man
Bow'd himself down, and in that mystery
Where God-in-man is one with man-in-God,
Pray'd for a blessing on his wife and babes,
Whatever came to him : and then he said
1.. " Annie, this voyage by the grace of God
Will bring fair weather yet to all of us.
Keep a clean hearth and a clean fire for me,
165
be dwe

For I 'll be back, my girl, before you know it."
Then lightly rocking baby's cradle, " and he,
195 This pretty, puny, weakly little one,—
Nay — for I love him all the better for it —
God bless him, he shall sit upon my knees
And I will tell him tales of foreign parts,
And make him merry, when I come home again.
200 Come, Annie, come, cheer up before I go.''

Him running on thus hopefully she heard,
And almost hoped herself; but when he turn'd
The current of his talk to graver things,
In sailor fashion roughly sermonizing
205 On providence and trust in Heaven, she heard,
Heard and not heard him; as the village girl,
Who sets her pitcher underneath the spring,
Musing on him that used to fill it for her,
Hears and not hears, and lets it overflow.

210 At length she spoke, " O Enoch, you are wise;
And yet for all your wisdom well know I
That I shall look upon your face no more."

" Well then," said Enoch, " I shall look on yours,
Annie, the ship I sail in passes here
215 (He named the day), get you a seaman's glass,
Spy out my face, and laugh at all your fears."

But when the last of those last moments came,
" Annie, my girl, cheer up, be comforted,
Look to the babes, and till I come again,
220 Keep everything shipshape, for I must go.
And fear no more for me: or if you fear

Cast all your cares on God ; that anchor holds.
Is He not yonder in those uttermost
Parts of the morning? if I flee to these
₂₂₅ Can I go from him? and the sea is His,
The sea is His: He made it."

                           Enoch rose,
Cast his strong arms about his drooping wife,
And kiss'd his wonder-stricken little ones ;
But for the third, the sickly one, who slept
₂₃₀ After a night of feverous wakefulness,
When Annie would have raised him Enoch said,
" Wake him not; let him sleep; how should the
        child
Remember this ? " and kiss'd him in his cot.
But Annie from her baby's forehead clipt
₂₃₅ A tiny curl, and gave it: this he kept
Thro' all his future ; but now hastily caught
His bundle, waved his hand, and went his way.

    She when the day, that Enoch mention'd, came,
Borrow'd a glass, but all in vain : perhaps
₂₄₀ She could not fix the glass to suit her eye ;
Perhaps her eye was dim, hand tremulous ;
She saw him not : and while he stood on deck
Waving, the moment and the vessel past.

    Ev'n to the last dip of the vanishing sail
₂₄₅ She watch'd it, and departed weeping for him :
Then, tho' she mourn'd his absence as his grave,
Set her sad will no less to chime with his,
But throve not in her trade, not being bred

To barter, nor compensating the want
150 By shrewdness, neither capable of lies,
Nor asking overmuch and taking less.
And still foreboding " what would Enoch say?"
For more than once, in days of difficulty
And pressure, had she sold her wares for less
255 Than what she gave in buying what she sold :
She fail'd and sadden'd knowing it : and thus,
Expectant of that news which never came,
Gain'd for her own a scanty sustenance,
And lived a life of silent melancholy.

260   Now the third child was sickly-born and grew
Yet sicklier, tho' the mother cared for it
With all a mother's care : nevertheless,
Whether her business often call'd her from it,
Or thro' the want of what it needed most,
265 Or means to pay the voice who best could tell
What most it needed — howsoe'er it was,
After a lingering, — ere she was aware, —
Like the caged bird escaping suddenly,
The little innocent soul flitted away.

270   In that same week when Annie buried it,
Philip's true heart, which hunger'd for her peace
(Since Enoch left he had not look'd upon her),
Smote him, as having kept aloof so long.
" Surely," said Philip, " I may see her now,
275 May be some little comfort ; " therefore went,
Past thro' the solitary room in front,
Paused for a moment at an inner door,
Then struck it thrice, and, no one opening,
Enter'd : but Annie, seated with her grief,

Cared not to look on any human face,
But turn'd her own toward the wall and wept.
Then Philip standing up said falteringly,
" Annie, I came to ask a favor of you."

285 He spoke: the passion in her moan'd reply,
" Favor from one so sad and so forlorn
As I am!" half abash'd him; yet unask'd,
His bashfulness and tenderness at war,
He set himself beside her, saying to her:

290 " I came to speak to you of what he wish'd,
Enoch, your husband: I have ever said
You chose the best among us — a strong man:
For where he fixt his heart he set his hand
To do the thing he will'd, and bore it thro'.
295 And wherefore did he go this weary way,
And leave you lonely? not to see the world —
For pleasure? — nay, but for the wherewithal
To give his babes a better bringing-up
Than his had been, or yours: that was his wish.
300 And if he come again, vext will he be
To find the precious morning hours were lost.
And it would vex him even in his grave,
If he could know his babes were running wild
Like colts about the waste. So, Annie, now —
305 Have we not known each other all our lives? —
I do beseech you by the love you bear
Him and his children not to say me nay —
For if you will, when Enoch comes again,
Why then he shall repay me — it you will,
310 Annie — for I am rich and well-to-do.
No

Then Annie with her brows against the wall
Answer'd, " I cannot look you in the face ;
315 I seem so foolish and so broken down.
When you came in my sorrow broke me down ;
And now I think your kindness breaks me down ;
But Enoch lives ; that is borne in on me ;
He will repay you : money can be repaid ;
320 Not kindness such as yours."

                              And Philip ask'd
"Then you will let me, Annie ? "

                              There she turn'd,
She rose, and fixt her swimming eyes upon him,
And dwelt a moment on his kindly face,
Then calling down a blessing on his head
325 Caught at his hand, and wrung it passionately,
And past into the little garth beyond.
So lifted up in spirit he moved away.

  Then Philip put the boy and girl to school,
And bought them needful books. and every way,
330 Like one who does his duty by his own.
Made himself theirs : and tho' for Annie's sake,
Fearing the lazy gossip of the port,
He oft denied his heart his dearest wish.
And seldom crost her threshold, yet he sent
335 Gifts by the children, garden-herbs and fruit,
The late and early roses from his wall,
Or conies from the down, and now and then,
With some pretext of fineness in the meal
To save the offence of charitable. flour
340 From his tall mill that whistled on the waste.

U

But Philip did not fathom Annie's mind:
Scarce could the woman when he came upon her,
Out of full heart and boundless gratitude
Light on a broken word to thank him with.
345 But Philip was her children's all-in-all;
From distant corners of the street they ran
To greet his hearty welcome heartily;
Lords of his house and of his mill were they;
Worried his passive ear with petty wrongs
350 Or pleasures, hung upon him, play'd with him,
And call'd him Father Philip. Philip gain'd
As Enoch lost; for Enoch seem'd to them
Uncertain as a vision or a dream,
Faint as a figure seen in early dawn
355 Down at the far end of an avenue,
Going we know not where: and so ten years,
Since Enoch left his hearth and native land,
Fled forward, and no news of Enoch came.

It chanced one evening Annie's children long'd
360 To go with others nutting to the wood,
And Annie would go with them; then they begg'd
For Father Philip (as they call'd him) too:
Him, like the working bee in blossom-dust,
Blanch'd with his mill, they found: and saying to him
365 "Come with us, Father Philip," he denied;
But when the children pluck'd at him to go,
He laugh'd, and yielded readily to their wish.
For was not Annie with them? and they went.

But after scaling half the weary down,
370 Just where the prone edge of the wood began

370 The repetition here of the phrase in line 67 is one of the
instances

To feather toward the hollow, all her force
Fail'd her ; and sighing, " Let me rest," she said
So Philip rested with her well-content :
While all the younger ones with jubilant cries
375 Broke from their elders, and tumultuously
Down thro' the whitening hazels made a plunge
To the bottom, and dispersed, and bent or broke
The lithe reluctant boughs to tear away
Their tawny clusters, crying to each other
380 And calling, here and there, about the wood.

　　But Philip sitting at her side forgot
Her presence, and remember'd one dark hour
Here in this wood, when like a wounded life
He crept into the shadow : at last he said,
385 Lifting his honest forehead, " Listen, Annie,
How merry they are down yonder in the wood.
Tired, Annie ? " for she did not speak a word.
" Tired ? " but her face had fall'n upon her hands ;
At which, as with a kind of anger in him,
390 " The ship was lost," he said, " the ship was lost !
No more of that ! why should you kill yourself
And make them orphans quite ? " And Annie said
" I thought not of it : but — I know not why —
Their voices make me feel so solitary."

395　　Then Philip coming somewhat closer spoke.
" Annie, there is a thing upon my mind,
And it has been upon my mind so long,
That tho' I know not when it first came there,
I know that it will out at last. Oh, Annie,
400 It is beyond all hope, against all chance,

two parts of the tragedy and make it all one   Compare lines
80 ;   id
U.

That he who left you ten long years ago
Should still be living; well then — let me speak:
I grieve to see you poor and wanting help:
I cannot help you as I wish to do
405 Unless — they say that women are so quick —
Perhaps you know what I would have you know —
I wish you for my wife. I fain would prove
A father to your children: I do think
They love me as a father: I am sure
410 That I love them as if they were mine own;
And I believe, if you were fast my wife,
That after all these sad uncertain years,
We might be still as happy as God grants
To any of His creatures. Think upon it:
415 For I am well-to-do — no kin, no care,
No burthen, save my care for you and yours:
And we have known each other all our lives,
And I have loved you longer than you know."

Then answer'd Annie: tenderly she spoke:
420 "You have been as God's good angel in our house.
God bless you for it, God reward you for it,
Philip, with something happier than myself.
Can one love twice? can you be ever loved
As Enoch was? what is it that you ask?"
425 "I am content," he answer'd, "to be loved
A little after Enoch." "Oh," she cried,
Scared as it were, "dear Philip, wait a while:
If Enoch comes — but Enoch will not come —
Yet wait a year, a year is not so long:
430 Surely I shall be wiser in a year:
Oh, wait a little!" Philip sadly said,
"Annie, as I have waited all my life
I well

" I am bound : you have my promise — in a year ;
435 Will you not bide your year as I bide mine ? "
And Philip answer'd. " I will bide my year."

Here both were mute, till Philip glancing up
Beheld the dead flame of the fallen day
Pass from the Danish barrow overhead ;
440 Then, fearing night and chill for Annie, rose,
And sent his voice beneath him thro' the wood.
Up came the children laden with their spoil ;
Then all descended to the port, and there
At Annie's door he paused and gave his hand,
445 Saying gently, " Annie, when I spoke to you,
That was your hour of weakness. I was wrong.
I am always bound to you, but you are free."
Then Annie weeping answered, " I am bound."

She spoke : and in one moment as it were,
450 While yet she went about her household ways,
Ev'n as she dwelt upon his latest words,
That he had loved her longer than she knew,
That autumn into autumn flash'd again,
And there he stood once more before her face,
455 Claiming her promise. " Is it a year ? " she ask'd.
" Yes, if the nuts," he said, " be ripe again :
Come out and see." But she — she put him off —
So much to look to — such a change — a month —
Give her a month — she knew that she was bound ·-
460 A month — no more. Then Philip with his eyes
Full of that lifelong hunger, and his voice
Shaking a little like a drunkard's hand,
" Take your own time, Annie, take your own time."
And Annie could have wept for pity of him ;
465 And yet she held him on delayingly

With many a scarce-believable excuse,
Trying his truth and his long-sufferance,
Till half another year had slipt away.

By this the lazy gossips of the port,
450 Abhorrent of a calculation crost,
Began to chafe as at a personal wrong.
Some thought that Philip did but trifle with her;
Some that she but held off to draw him on ;
And others laugh'd at her and Philip too,
455 As simple folk that knew not their own minds ;
And one, in whom all evil fancies clung
Like serpent eggs together, laughingly
Would hint at worse in either. Her own son
Was silent, tho' he often look'd his wish :
460 But evermore the daughter prest upon her
To wed the man so dear to all of them
And lift the household out of poverty ;
And Philip's rosy face contracting grew
Careworn and wan ; and all these things fell on h
465 Sharp as reproach.

At last one night it chanced
That Annie could not sleep, but earnestly
Pray'd for a sign. " my Enoch, is he gone? "
Then compass'd round by the blind wall of night
Brook'd not the expectant terror of her heart,
470 Started from bed, and struck herself a light,
Then desperately seized the holy Book,

---

470 Angry that their expectations were not fulfilled
491. From early times one form of divination has been
read a personal meaning in passages selected by chance
books. The Lord of [...] was often used, and in [...]
the [...]

Suddenly set it wide to find a sign,
Suddenly put her finger on the text,
" Under the palm-tree." That was nothing to her :
495 No meaning there : she closed the Book and slept :
When lo! her Enoch sitting on a height,
Under a palm-tree, over him the Sun :
" He is gone," she thought, " he is happy, he is
    singing
Hosanna in the highest: yonder shines
500 The Sun of Righteousness, and these be palms
Whereof the happy people strowing cried
' Hosanna in the highest! ' " Here she woke,
Resolved, sent for him and said wildly to him,
" There is no reason why we should not wed."
505 " Then for God's sake," he answer'd, " both our
    sakes,
So you will wed me, let it be at once."

    So these were wed and merrily rang the bells,
Merrily rang the bells and they were wed.
But never merrily beat Annie's heart.
510 A footstep seem'd to fall beside her path,
She knew not whence ; a whisper on her ear,
She knew not what : nor loved she to be left
Alone at home, nor ventured out alone.
What ail'd her then, that ere she enter'd, often,
515 Her hand dwelt lingeringly on the latch,
Fearing to enter : Philip thought he knew

Such doubts and fears were common to her state,
Annie, since the days of the Puritans In George Eliot's
Adam Bede, Dinah Morris makes important use of the practice.
' And when I've opened the Bible for direction," she says,
" I ve always lighted on some clear word to tell me where
my work lay "

Being with child : but when her child was born,
Then her new child was as herself renew'd,
520 Then the new mother came about her **heart**,
Then her good Philip was her all-**in-all**,
And that mysterious instinct wholly died.

   And where was Enoch? prosperously sail'd
The ship Good Fortune, tho' at setting forth
525 The Biscay, roughly ridging eastward, shook
And almost overwhelm'd her, yet unvext
She slipt across the summer of the world,
Then after a long tumble about the Cape
And frequent interchange of foul and fair,
530 She passing thro' the summer world again,
The breath of heaven came continually
And sent her sweetly by the golden isles,
Till silent in her oriental haven.

   There Enoch traded for himself, and bought
535 Quaint monsters for the market of those times,
A gilded dragon, also, for the babes.

   Less lucky her home-voyage : at first indeed
Thro' many a fair sea-circle, day by day,
Scarce-rocking her full-busted figure-head
540 Stared o'er the ripple feathering from her bows :
Then follow'd calms, and then winds variable,
Then baffling, a long course of them ; and last
Storm, such as drove her under moonless heavens
Till hard upon the cry of " breakers " came

527 This of course refers to the region about the equator
537 **Voyage** here is more nearly one syllable
538 Tl
centr

545 The crash of ruin, and the loss of all
But Enoch and two others.   Half the night,
Buoy'd upon floating tackle and broken spars,
These drifted, stranding on an isle at morn
Rich, but the loneliest in a lonely sea.

550   No want was there of human sustenance,
Soft fruitage, mighty nuts, and nourishing roots;
Nor save for pity was it hard to take
The helpless life so wild that it was tame.
There in a seaward-gazing mountain-gorge
555 They built, and thatch'd with leaves of palm, a hut,
Half hut, half native cavern.   So the three,
Set in this Eden of all plenteousness,
Dwelt with eternal summer, ill-content.

For one, the youngest, hardly more than boy,
560 Hurt in that night of sudden ruin and wreck,
Lay lingering out a five-years' death-in-life.
They could not leave him.   After he was gone,
The two remaining found a fallen stem;
And Enoch's comrade, careless of himself,
565 Fire-hollowing this in Indian fashion, fell
Sun-stricken, and that other lived alone.
In those two deaths he read God's warning, " Wait."

The mountain wooded to the peak, the lawns
And winding glades high up like ways to Heaven,
570 The slender coco's drooping crown of plumes,
The lightning flash of insect and of bird,
The lustre of the long convolvuluses'
That coil'd around the stately stems, and ran
Ev'n to the limit of the land, the glows

575 And glories of the broad belt of the world,
All these he saw; but what he fain had seen
He could not see, the kindly human face,
Nor ever hear a kindly voice, but heard
The myriad shriek of wheeling ocean-fowl,
580 The league-long roller thundering on the reef.
The moving whisper of huge trees that branch'd
And blossom'd in the zenith, or the sweep
Of some precipitous rivulet to the wave,
As down the shore he ranged, or all day long
585 Sat often in the seaward-gazing gorge,
A shipwreck'd sailor, waiting for a sail:
No sail from day to day, but every day
The sunrise broken into scarlet shafts
Among the palms and ferns and precipices;
590 The blaze upon the waters to the east:
The blaze upon his island overhead;
The blaze upon the waters to the west;
Then the great stars that globed themselves in
         Heaven,
The hollower-bellowing ocean, and again
595 The scarlet shafts of sunrise — but no sail.

There often as he watch'd or seem'd to watch,
So still, the golden lizard on him paused,
A phantom made of many phantoms moved
Before him, haunting him, or he himself
600 Moved haunting people, things and places, known
Far in a darker isle beyond the line;
The babes, their babble, Annie, the small house,
The climbing street, the mill, the leafy lanes,

575 Broad belt of the world, the ocean; the ancients, indeed, had
597. *the*

The peacock-yewtree and the lonely Hall.
305 The horse he drove, the boat he sold, the chill
November dawns and dewy-glooming downs,
The gentle shower, the smell of dying leaves,
And the low moan of leaden-color'd seas.

Once likewise, in the ringing of his ears,
310 Tho' faintly, merrily — far and far away —
He heard the pealing of his parish bells;
Then, tho' he knew not wherefore, started up
Shuddering, and when the beauteous hateful isle
Return'd upon him, had not his poor heart
315 Spoken with That, which being everywhere
Lets none who speaks with Him seem all alone,
Surely the man had died of solitude.

Thus over Enoch's early-silvering head
The sunny and rainy seasons came and went
320 Year after year. His hopes to see his own,
And pace the sacred old familiar fields,
Not yet had perish'd, when his lonely doom
Came suddenly to an end. Another ship
(She wanted water) blown by baffling winds,
325 Like the Good Fortune, from her destined course,
Stay'd by this isle, not knowing where she lay:
For since the mate had seen at early dawn
Across a break on the mist-wreathen isle
The silent water slipping from the hills,
330 They sent a crew that landing burst away
In search of stream or fount, and fill'd the shores
With clamor. Downward from his mountain gorge
Stept the long-hair'd, long-bearded solitary,
Brown, looking hardly human, strangely clad,

With inarticulate rage, and making signs
They knew not what: and yet he led the way
To where the rivulets of sweet water ran;
And ever as he mingled with the crew,
And heard them talking, his long-bounden tongue
Was loosen'd, till he made them understand,
Whom, when their casks were fill'd they took
        aboard
And there the tale he utter'd brokenly,
Scarce-credited at first but more and more,
Amazed and melted all who listen'd to it;
And clothes they gave him and free passage home;
But oft he work'd among the rest and shook
His isolation from him.   None of these
Came from his county, or could answer him,
If question'd, aught of what he cared to know.
And dull the voyage was with long delays,
The vessel scarce sea-worthy; but evermore
His fancy fled before the lazy wind
Returning, till beneath a clouded moon
He like a lover down thro' all his blood
Drew in the dewy meadowy morning-breath
Of England, blown across her ghostly wall:
And that same morning officers and men
Levied a kindly tax upon themselves,
Pitying the lonely man, and gave him it:
Then moving up the coast they landed him,
Ev'n in that harbor whence he sail'd before.

    There Enoch spoke no word to any one,
But homeward — home — what home? had he ..
        home? —

638 Sweet water . . .
651 Voy
957 Hei

665 His home. he walk'd. Bright was that afternoon,
Sunny but chill ; till drawn thro' either chasm,
Where either haven open'd on the deeps,
Roll'd a sea-haze and whelm'd the world in gray ;
Cut off the length of highway on before,
670 And left but narrow breadth to left and right
Of wither'd holt or tilth or pasturage.
On the nigh-naked tree the robin piped
Disconsolate, and thro' the dripping haze
The dead weight of the dead leaf bore it down :
675 Thicker the drizzle grew, deeper the gloom :
Last, as it seem'd, a great mist-blotted light
Flared on him, and he came upon the place.

Then down the long street having slowly stolen,
His heart foreshadowing all calamity,
680 His eyes upon the stones, he reach'd the home
Where Annie lived and loved him, and his babes
In those far-off seven happy years were born ;
But finding neither light nor murmur there
(A bill of sale gleam'd thro' the drizzle) crept
685 Still downward thinking, " dead, or dead to me! "

Down to the pool and narrow wharf he went,
Seeking a tavern which of old he knew,
A front of timber-crost antiquity,
So propt, worm-eaten, ruinously old,
690 He thought it must have gone : but he was gone
Who kept it : and his widow, Miriam Lane,
With daily-dwindling profits held the house ;

667. See line 102

688 A house of plaster crossed with timbers, ' half-tim-
'ered " as it is called ; a style of architecture made familiar by

A haunt of brawling seamen once, but now
Stiller, with yet a bed for wandering men.
695 There Enoch rested silent many days.

But Miriam Lane was good and garrulous,
Nor let him be, but often breaking in,
Told him, with other annals of the port,
Not knowing — Enoch was so brown, so bow'd,
700 So broken — all the story of his house.
His baby's death, her growing poverty,
How Philip put her little ones to school,
And kept them in it, his long wooing her,
Her slow consent, and marriage, and the birth
705 Of Philip's child: and o'er his countenance
No shadow past, nor motion: any one,
Regarding, well had deem'd he felt the tale
Less than the teller; only when she closed,
" Enoch, poor man, was cast away and lost,"
710 He, shaking his gray head pathetically,
Repeated muttering, " cast away and lost ; "
Again in deeper inward whispers, " lost! "

But Enoch yearned to see her face again ;
" If I might look on her sweet face again
715 And know that she is happy." So the thought
Haunted and harass'd him, and drove him forth,
At evening when the dull November day
Was growing duller twilight, to the hill
There he sat down gazing on all below ;
720 There did a thousand memories roll upon him,
Unspeakable for sadness. By and by
The ruddy square of comfort, like light,
Fair . . . .
All . . .

725 The bird of passage, till he madly strikes
   Against it, and beats out his weary life.

   For Philip's dwelling fronted on the street,
   The latest house to landward; but behind,
   With one small gate that open'd on the waste,
730 Flourish'd a little garden square and wall'd:
   And in it throve an ancient evergreen,
   A yewtree, and all round it ran a walk
   Of shingle, and a walk divided it:
   But Enoch shunn'd the middle walk and stole
735 Up by the wall. behind the yew; and thence
   That which he better might have shunn'd, if griefs
   Like his have worse or better, Enoch saw.

   For cups and silver on the burnish'd board
   Sparkled and shone; so genial was the hearth:
740 And on the right hand of the hearth he saw
   Philip, the slighted suitor of old times,
   Stout, rosy, with his babe across his knees;
   And o'er her second father stoopt a girl,
   A later but a loftier Annie Lee,
745 Fair-hair'd and tall. and from her lifted hand
   Dangled a length of ribbon and a ring
   To tempt the babe. who rear'd his creasy arms,
   Caught at. and ever miss'd it, and they laugh'd:
   And on the left hand of the hearth he saw
750 The mother glancing often toward her babe.
   But turning now and then to speak with him.
   Her son, who stood beside her tall and strong,
   And saying that which pleased him, for he smiled

   728. Latest, last.
   733. Shingle, gravel from the seashore.

U.

Now when the dead man come to life beheld
155 His wife his wife no more, and saw the babe
Hers, yet not his, upon the father's knee,
And all the warmth, the peace, the happiness,
And his own children tall and beautiful,
And him, that other, reigning in his place,
160 Lord of his rights and of his children's love, —
Then he, tho' Miriam Lane had told him all,
Because things seen are mightier than things heard,
Stagger'd and shook, holding the branch, and fear'd
To send abroad a shrill and terrible cry,
165 Which in one moment, like the blast of doom,
Would shatter all the happiness of the hearth.

He therefore turning softly like a thief,
Lest the harsh shingle should grate underfoot,
And feeling all along the garden wall,
170 Lest he should swoon and tumble and be found,
Crept to the gate, and open'd it, and closed,
As lightly as a sick man's chamber-door,
Behind him, and came out upon the waste.

And there he would have knelt, but that his knees
175 Were feeble, so that falling prone he dug
His fingers into the wet earth, and pray'd.

"Too hard to bear! why did they take me thence,
O God Almighty, blessed Saviour, Thou
That didst uphold me on my lonely isle,
180 Uphold me, Father, in my loneliness
A little longer! aid me, give me strength
Not to tell her, never to let her know.
Help m
My ch

785 They know me not.   I should betray myself.
    Never: no father's kiss for me — the girl
    So like her mother, and the boy. my son."

    There speech and thought and nature fail'd a little
    And he lay tranced ; but when he rose and paced
790 Back toward his solitary home again,
    All down the long and narrow street he went
    Beating it in upon his weary brain,
    As tho' it were the burthen of a song,
    " Not to tell her. never to let her know."

795   He was not all unhappy.   His resolve
    Upbore him, and firm faith. and evermore
    Prayer from a living source within the will,
    And beating up thro' all the bitter world,
    Like fountains of sweet water in the sea.
800 Kept him a living soul.   " This miller's wife."
    He said to Miriam, " that you spoke about.
    Has she no fear that her first husband lives ?"
    " Ay, ay, poor soul,' said Miriam. " fear enow !
    If you could tell her you had seen him dead.
805 Why. that would be her comfort ." and he thought
    " After the Lord has call'd me she shall know,
    I wait His time ;" and Enoch set himself.
    Scorning an alms, to work whereby to live
    Almost to all things could he turn his hand
810 Cooper he was and carpenter. and wrought
    To make the boatmen fishing-nets, or help'd
    At lading and unlading the tall barks.
    That brought the stinted commerce of those days ;
    Thus earn'd a scanty living for himself :
815 Yet since he did but labor for himself.

Work without hope, there was not life in it
Whereby the man could live: and as the year
Roll'd itself round again to meet the day
When Enoch had return'd, a languor came
820 Upon him, gentle sickness, gradually
Weakening the man, till he could do no more,
But kept the house, his chair, and last his bed.
And Enoch bore his weakness cheerfully.
For sure no gladlier does the stranded wreck
825 See thro' the gray skirts of a lifting squall
The boat that bears the hope of life approach
To save the life despair'd of, than he saw
Death dawning on him, and the close of all.

For thro' that dawning gleam'd a kindlier hope
830 On Enoch thinking, "after I am gone,
Then may she learn I lov'd her to the last."
He call'd aloud for Miriam Lane and said
"Woman, I have a secret--only swear,
Before I tell you — swear upon the book
835 Not to reveal it, till you see me dead."
"Dead," clamor'd the good woman, "hear him talk;
I warrant, man, that we shall bring you round."
"Swear," added Enoch sternly, "on the book."
And on the book, half-frighted, Miriam swore.
840 Then Enoch rolling his gray eyes upon her,
"Did you know Enoch Arden of this town?"
"Know him?" she said, "I knew him far away.
Ay, ay, I mind him coming down the street;
Held his head high, and cared for no man, he."
845 Slowly and sadly Enoch answer'd her:
"His head is low, and no man cares for him
I think . . .
. . . . .

A half-incredulous, half-hysterical cry.
850 " You Arden, you! nay,— sure he was a foot
Higher than you be." Enoch said again
" My God has bow'd me down to what I am;
My grief and solitude have broken me;
Nevertheless, know you that I am he
855 Who married — but that name has twice been
    changed —
I married her who married Philip Ray.
Sit, listen." Then he told her of his voyage,
His wreck, his lonely life, his coming back,
His gazing in on Annie, his resolve,
860 And how he kept it. As the woman heard,
Fast flow'd the current of her easy tears,
While in her heart she yearn'd incessantly
To rush abroad all round the little haven,
Proclaiming Enoch Arden and his woes;
865 But awed and promise-bounden she forbore,
Saying only, " See your bairns before you go!
Eh, let me fetch 'em, Arden," and arose
Eager to bring them down, for Enoch hung
A moment on her words, but then replied.

870 " Woman, disturb me not now at the last,
But let me hold my purpose till I die.
Sit down again; mark me and understand,
While I have power to speak. I charge you now
When you shall see her, tell her that I died
875 Blessing her, praying for her, loving her:
Save for the bar between us, loving her
As when she lay her head beside my own,
And tell my daughter Anna, whom I saw

865. Bounden an old form of *bound* here used doubtless,
in [?]

So like her mother, that my latest breath
350 Was spent in blessing her and praying for her.
And tell my son that I died blessing him.
And say to Philip that I blest him too:
He never meant us any thing but good.
But if my children care to see me dead,
355 Who hardly knew me living, let them come,
I am their father; but she must not come,
For my dead face would vex her after-life.
And now there is but one of all my blood,
Who will embrace me in the world-to-be:
360 This hair is his: she cut it off and gave it,
And I have borne it with me all these years,
And thought to bear it with me to my grave;
But now my mind is changed, for I shall see him,
My babe in bliss: wherefore when I am gone,
365 Take, give her this, for it may comfort her:
It will moreover be a token to her,
That I am he."

        He ceased: and Miriam Lane
Made such a voluble answer promising all,
That once again he roll'd his eyes upon her
370 Repeating all he wish'd, and once again
She promised.

        Then the third night after this,
While Enoch slumber'd motionless and pale,
And Miriam watch'd and dozed at intervals,
There came so loud a calling of the sea,
375 That all the houses in the haven rang.
He woke, he rose, he spread his arms abroad
Crying
I am

So past the strong heroic soul away.
910 And when they buried him the little port
Had seldom seen a costlier funeral.

THE DAY-DREAM.

PROLOGUE.

O LADY FLORA, let me speak:
A pleasant hour has past away
While, dreaming on your damask cheek,
The dewy sister-eyelids lay.
5 As by the lattice you reclined,
I went thro' many wayward moods
To see you dreaming — and, behind,
A summer crisp with shining woods.
And I too dream'd, until at last
10   Across my fancy, brooding warm,
The reflex of a legend past,
And loosely settled into form.

911. The good taste of calling attention to the costliness of
Enoch's funeral has been questioned, but is not the fact that
expense would signify more than any other one thing to the
villagers a sufficient explanation, or must we look for some sub-
tler additional reference to what the event cost in Annie's life?

The Day-Dream The germ of *The Day Dream* is to be found
in *The Sleeping Beauty*, which first appeared in the volume of
1830. In its expanded, complete form the poem became a part
of the volume of 1842. It is one of the best instances in English literature of the giving of new life, through a new form of
beauty, to an old tale. The device of making a personal setting for his story — here by addressing it and its application to
" Lady Flora" — was a favorite one with Tennyson. In the first
form of the *Morte d' Arthur* called *The Epic*, and in *The Princess*
this method may be observed.

                                                    Twelfth

And would you have the thought I had,
    And see the vision that I saw,
15 Then take the broidery-frame, and add
    A crimson to the quaint macaw,
And I will tell it. Turn your face,
    Nor look with that too-earnest eye —
The rhymes are dazzled from their place,
20   And order'd words asunder fly.

THE SLEEPING PALACE.

I.

The varying year with blade and sheaf
    Clothes and reclothes the happy plains,
Here rests the sap within the leaf,
    Here stays the blood among the veins.
25 Faint shadows, vapors lightly curl'd,
    Faint murmurs from the meadows come,
Like hints and echoes of the world
    To spirits folded in the womb.

II.

Soft lustre bathes the range of urns
30   On every slanting terrace-lawn.
The fountain to his place returns
    Deep in the garden lake withdrawn.
Here droops the banner on the tower,
    On the hall-hearths the festal fires,
35 The peacock in his laurel bower,
    The parrot in his gilded wires.

U.

III.

Roof-haunting martins warm their eggs:
  In these, in those the life is stay'd.
The mantles from the golden pegs
40 Droop sleepily: no sound is made,
Not even of a gnat that sings.
  More like a picture seemeth all
Than those old portraits of old kings,
  That watch the sleepers from the wall.

IV.

45 Here sits the butler with a flask
  Between his knees, half-drain'd; and there
The wrinkled steward at his task.
  The maid-of-honor blooming fair;
The page has caught her hand in his:
50 Her lips are sever'd as to speak:
His own are pouted to a kiss:
  The blush is fix'd upon her cheek.

V.

Till all the hundred summers pass.
  The beams, that thro' the oriel shine,
55 Make prisms in every carven glass,
  And beaker brimm'd with noble wine.
Each baron at the banquet sleeps.
  Grave faces gather'd in a ring.
His state the king reposing keeps.
60 He must have been a jovial king.

37. **Martins** Shakespeare's "temple-haunting martlet" in
Macbeth is the same bird, — a swallow.

VI.

All round a hedge upshoots, and shows
   At distance like a little wood :
Thorns, ivies, woodbine, mistletoes,
   And grapes with bunches red as blood ;
65 All creeping plants, a wall of green
   Close-matted, bur and brake and brier,
And glimpsing over these, just seen,
   High up, the topmost palace-spire.

VII.

When will the hundred summers die,
70   And thought and time be born again,
And newer knowledge, drawing nigh,
   Bring truth that sways the soul of men?
Here all things in their place remain,
   As all were order'd, ages since.
75 Come, Care and Pleasure, Hope and Pain,
   And bring the fated fairy Prince.

THE SLEEPING BEAUTY.

I.

Year after year unto her feet,
   She lying on her couch alone,
Across the purple coverlet,
80   The maiden's jet-black hair has grown,
On either side her tranced form
   Forth streaming from a braid of pearl :
The slumbrous light is rich and warm,

II.

85 The silk star-broider'd coverlid
      Unto her limbs itself doth mould
   Languidly ever ; and, amid
      Her full black ringlets downward roll'd,
   Glows forth each softly-shadow'd arm
30   With bracelets of the diamond bright :
   Her constant beauty doth inform
      Stillness with love, and day with light.

III.

   She sleeps : her breathings are not heard
      In palace chambers far apart.
95 The fragrant tresses are not stirr'd
      That lie upon her charmèd heart.
   She sleeps : on either hand upswells
      The gold-fringed pillow lightly prest :
   She sleeps, nor dreams, but ever dwells
100   A perfect form in perfect rest.

THE ARRIVAL.

I.

   All precious things, discover'd late,
      To those that seek them issue forth,
   For love in sequel works with fate,
      And draws the veil from hidden worth.
5 He travels far from other skies —
      His mantle glitters on the rocks —
   A fairy Prince, with joyful eyes,
      And lighter-footed than the fox.

U.

II.

The bodies and the bones of those
10   That strove in other days to pass,
  Are wither'd in the thorny close,
    Or scatter'd blanching on the grass.
He gazes on the silent dead:
    "They perish'd in their daring deeds."
15 This proverb flashes thro' his head,
    "The many fail: the one succeeds."

III.

He comes, scarce knowing what he seeks:
  He breaks the hedge: he enters there:
  The color flies into his cheeks:
20   He trusts to light on something fair;
For all his life the charm did talk
  About his path, and hover near
With words of promise in his walk,
    And whisper'd voices at his ear.

IV.

25 More close and close his footsteps wind:
  The magic music in his heart
Beats quick and quicker, till he find
  The quiet chamber far apart.
His spirit flutters like a lark,
30   He stoops — to kiss her — on his knee.
  "Love, if thy tresses be so dark
    How dark those hidden eyes must be!'

11 The thorny close   See lines of 66
121, 126 The charm and the magic music are what well
may have

THE REVIVAL.

I.

A touch, a kiss! the charm was snapt.
  There rose a noise of striking clocks,
135 And feet that ran, and doors that clapt,
  And barking dogs, and crowing cocks;
A fuller light illumined all,
  A breeze thro' all the garden swept,
A sudden hubbub shook the hall,
140   And sixty feet the fountain leapt.

II.

The hedge broke in, the banner blew,
  The butler drank, the steward scrawl'd,
The fire shot up, the martin flew.
  The parrot scream'd, the peacock squall'd,
145 The maid and page renew'd their strife,
  The palace bang'd and buzz'd and clackt,
And all the long-pent stream of life
  Dash'd downward in a cataract.

III.

And last with these the king awoke.
150   And in his chair himself uprear'd,
And yawn'd, and rubb'd his face, and spoke,
  " By holy rood, a royal beard!
How say you? we have slept, my lords.
  My beard has grown into my lap."
155 The barons swore, with many words,
  'T was but an after-dinner's nap.

152. **Rood** = the cross; a common oath in ancient England.

U.

IV.

"Pardy," return'd the king, "but still
　My joints are somewhat stiff or so.
My lord. and shall we pass the bill
160　I mention'd half an hour ago?"
The chancellor, sedate and vain,
　In courteous words return'd reply:
But dallied with his golden chain,
　And, smiling, put the question by.

THE DEPARTURE.

I.

165 And on her lover's arm she leant,
　And round her waist she felt it fold,
And far across the hills they went
　In that new world which is the old:
Across the hills, and far away
170　Beyond their utmost purple rim,
And deep into the dying day
　The happy princess follow'd him.

II.

"I'd sleep another hundred years,
　O love, for such another kiss:"
175 "O wake for ever, love," she hears.
　"O love, 't was such as this and this."
And o'er them many a sliding star,
　And many a merry wind was borne,
And, stream'd thro' many a golden bar,
180

157　P²
(by God)

III.

"O eyes long laid in happy sleep!"
    "O happy sleep, that lightly fled!"
"O happy kiss, that woke thy sleep!"
    "O love, thy kiss would wake the dead!"
185 And o'er them many a flowing range
    Of vapor buoy'd the crescent-bark,
And, rapt thro' many a rosy change,
    The twilight died into the dark.

IV.

"A hundred summers! can it be?
190   And whither goest thou, tell me where?"
"O seek my father's court with me,
    For there are greater wonders there."
And o'er the hills, and far away
    Beyond their utmost purple rim,
195 Beyond the night, across the day,
    Thro' all the world she follow'd him.

MORAL.

I.

So, Lady Flora, take my lay,
    And if you find no moral there,
Go, look in any glass and say,
200   What moral is in being fair.
Oh, to what uses shall we put
    The wildweed-flower that simply blows?
And is there any moral shut
    Within the bosom of the rose?

U,   . '   .   likened
to

II.

205 But any man that walks the mead,
 In bud or blade, or bloom, may find,
According as his humors lead,
 A meaning suited to his mind.
And liberal applications lie
210 In Art like Nature, dearest friend;
So 't were to cramp its use, if I
 Should hook it to some useful end.

L'ENVOI.

I.

You shake your head.   A random string
 Your finer female sense offends.
215 Well — were it not a pleasant thing
 To fall asleep with all one's friends;
To pass with all our social ties
 To silence from the paths of men:
And every hundred years to rise
220 And learn the world, and sleep again;
To sleep thro' terms of mighty wars,
 And wake on science grown to more,
On secrets of the brain, the stars,
 As wild as aught of fairy lore:
225 And all that else the years will show,
 The Poet-forms of stronger hours,
The vast Republics that may grow,
 The Federations and the Powers;
Titanic forces taking birth

213 A
moral U.

230   In divers seasons, divers climes?
For we are Ancients of the earth,
   And in the morning of the times.

II.

So sleeping, so aroused from sleep
   Thro' sunny decades new and strange,
235 Or gay quinquenniads would we reap
   The flower and quintessence of change.

III.

Ah, yet would I — and would I might!
   So much your eyes my fancy take —
Be still the first to leap to light
240   That I might kiss those eyes awake!
For, am I right or am I wrong,
   To choose your own you did not care;
You 'd have *my* moral from the song,
   And I will take my pleasure there;
245 And, am I right or am I wrong,
   My fancy, ranging thro' and thro',
To search a meaning for the song,
   Perforce will still revert to you;
Nor finds a closer truth than this
250   All-graceful head, so richly curl'd,
And evermore a costly kiss
   The prelude to some brighter world.

IV.

For since the time when Adam first
   Embraced his Eve in happy hour,
255 And every bird of Eden burst

235. Quinquenniads — periods of five years

                       able.

In carol, every bud to flower,
What eyes, like thine, have waken'd hopes?
    What lips, like thine, so sweetly join'd?
Where on the double rosebud droops
60   The fullness of the pensive mind;
Which all too dearly self-involved,
    Yet sleeps a dreamless sleep to me;
A sleep by kisses undissolved,
    That lets thee neither hear nor see:
265 But break it.   In the name of wife,
    And in the rights that name may give,
Are clasp'd the moral of thy life.
    And that for which I care to live.

EPILOGUE.

So, Lady Flora, take my lay,
270   And, if you find a meaning there,
O whisper to your glass, and say,
    "What wonder, if he thinks me fair?"
What wonder I was all unwise,
    To shape the song for your delight
275 Like long-tail'd birds of Paradise,
    That float thro' Heaven, and cannot light?
Or old-world trains, upheld at court
    By Cupid-boys of blooming hue —
But take it — earnest wed with sport,
280   And either sacred unto you.

259 The double rosebud of course the lips of the line
before
277 Old-world trains the long skirts of old-world dresses

U.

DORA.

WITH farmer Allan at the farm abode
William and Dora. William was his son,
And she his niece. He often looked at them,
And often thought, " I 'll make them man and wife."
5 Now Dora felt her uncle's will in all,
And yearn'd towards William ; but the youth, be-
cause
He had been always with her in the house,
Thought not of Dora.
                              Then there came a day
When Allan call'd his son, and said. " My son :
10 I married late, but I would wish to see
My grandchild on my knees before I die :
And I have set my heart upon a match.
Now therefore look to Dora ; she is well
To look to ; thrifty too beyond her age.
15 She is my brother's daughter : he and I
Had once hard words, and parted, and he died
In foreign lands : but for his sake I bred
His daughter Dora : take her for your wife :
For I have wish'd this marriage, night and day,
20 For many years.'   But William answer'd short :
" I cannot marry Dora : by my life.

Dora is one of the poems which, according to a plan Tennyson
formed and abandoned for the title of one of his books, might
well have been called an *Idyll of the Hearth*. It first appeared
in the two-volume Edition of 1842. Such is the simplicity of
the poem in plan and diction that " notes " are more than usually
a superfluity.

    To the story of " Dora Creswell," in Miss Mitford's *Our Vil-
lage* Tennyson acknowledged his debt for the origin of the
poem   losely,
evi   ps the
mo

I will not marry Dora." Then the old man
Was wroth, and doubled up his hands, and said:
" You will not, boy! you dare to answer thus!
25 But in my time a father's word was law,
And so it shall be now for me. Look to it;
Consider, William: take a month to think,
And let me have an answer to my wish:
Or, by the Lord that made me, you shall pack,
30 And never more darken my doors again"
But William answer'd madly: bit his lips,
And broke away. The more he look'd at her
The less he liked her; and his ways were harsh:
But Dora bore them meekly. Then before
35 The month was out he left his father's house,
And hired himself to work within the fields:
And half in love, half spite, he woo'd and wed
A laborer's daughter, Mary Morrison.
    Then, when the bells were ringing, Allan call'd
40 His niece and said: " My girl, I love you well;
But if you speak with him that was my son,
Or change a word with her he calls his wife,
My home is none of yours. My will is law."
And Dora promised, being meek. She thought,
45 " It cannot be: my uncle's mind will change!"
    And days went on, and there was born a boy
To William: then distresses came on him:
And day by day he pass'd his father's gate,
Heart-broken, and his father help'd him not.
50 But Dora stored what little she could save,
And sent it them by stealth, nor did they know
Who sent it: till at last a town that seized
On William, and in harvest time he died.
55 And

Hard things of Dora. Dora came and said:
  "I have obey'd my uncle until now,
And I have sinn'd, for it was all thro' me
This evil came on William at the first.
80 But, Mary, for the sake of him that 's gone,
And for your sake, the woman that he chose,
And for this orphan, I am come to you:
You know there has not been for these five years
So full a harvest: let me take the boy,
85 And I will set him in my uncle's eye
Among the wheat; that when his heart is glad
Of the full harvest, he may see the boy,
And bless him for the sake of him that 's gone."
  And Dora took the child. and went her way
70 Across the wheat. and sat upon a mound
That was unsown, where many poppies grew.
Far off the farmer came into the field
And spied her not; for none of all his men
Dare tell him Dora waited with the child;
75 And Dora would have risen and gone to him,
But her heart fail'd her, and the reapers reap'd,
And the sun fell, and all the land was dark.
  But when the morrow came. she rose and took
The child once more, and sat upon the mound;
80 And made a little wreath of all the flowers
That grew about, and tied it round his hat
To make him pleasing in her uncle's eye.
Then when the farmer pass'd into the field
He spied her. and he left his men at work,
85 And came and said: "Where were you yesterday?
Whose child is that? What are you doing here?"
So Dora cast her eyes upon the ground,
And answer'd softly. "This is William's child!"

" Do with me as you will, but take the child,
And bless him for the sake of him that 's gone ! "
And Allan said, " I see it is a trick
Got up betwixt you and the woman there.
95 I must be taught my duty, and by you !
You knew my word was law, and yet you dared
To slight it.   Well — for I will take the boy ;
But go you hence, and never see me more."
   So saying, he took the boy, that cried aloud
100 And struggled hard.   The wreath of flowers fell
At Dora's feet.   She bow'd upon her hands,
And the boy's cry came to her from the field,
More and more distant.   She bow'd down her head,
Remembering the day when first she came,
105 And all the things that had been.   She bow'd down
And wept in secret ; and the reapers reap'd,
And the sun fell, and all the land was dark.
   Then Dora went to Mary's house, and stood
Upon the threshold.   Mary saw the boy
110 Was not with Dora.   She broke out in praise
To God, that help'd her in her widowhood.
And Dora said, " My uncle took the boy ;
But, Mary, let me live and work with you :
He says that he will never see me more."
115 Then answer'd Mary, " This shall never be,
That thou shouldst take my trouble on thyself :
And, now I think, he shall not have the boy,
For he will teach him hardness, and to slight
His mother : therefore thou and I will go,
120 And I will have my boy, and bring him home ;
And I will beg of him to take thee back :
But if he will not take thee back again,
Then
And
125 Of age to help us.

So the women kiss'd
Each other, and set out, and reach'd the farm.
The door was off the latch : they peep'd, and saw
The boy set up betwixt his grandsire's knees,
Who thrust him in the hollows of his arm,
'30 And clapt him on the hands and on the cheeks,
Like one that loved him : and the lad stretch'd out
And babbled for the golden seal, that hung
From Allan s watch, and sparkled by the fire.
Then they came in : but when the boy beheld
135 His mother, he cried out to come to her :
And Allan set him down, and Mary said :
    " O Father! — if you let me call you so —
I never came a-begging for myself,
Or William, or this child : but now I come
10 For Dora : take her back ; she loves you well.
O Sir, when William died, he died at peace
With all men ; for I ask'd him, and he said,
He could not ever rue his marrying me —
I had been a patient wife, but, Sir, he said
145 That he was wrong to cross his father thus :
' God bless him !' he said, 'and may he never know
The troubles I have gone thro'!' Then he turn'd
His face and pass'd — unhappy that I am !
But now, Sir, let me have my boy, for you
150 Will make him hard, and he will learn to slight
His father's memory : and take Dora back,
And let all this be as it was before."
    So Mary said, and Dora hid her face
By Mary. There was silence in the room :
155 And all at once the old man burst in sobs : —

118 **Pass'd** this old use of *pass'd* for *died* is the same as in
the

"I have been to blame — to blame. I have kill'd
   my son.
I have kill'd him — but I loved him — my dear son.
May God forgive me! — I have been to blame.
Kiss me, my children."
                Then they clung about
160 The old man's neck, and kiss'd him many times.
And all the man was broken with remorse;
And all his love came back a hundredfold;
And for three hours he sobb'd o'er William's child,
Thinking of William.
              So those four abode
165 Within one house together: and as years
Went forward, Mary took another mate;
But Dora lived unmarried till her death.

THE TALKING OAK.

ONCE more the gate behind me falls,
   Once more before my face
I see the moulder'd Abbey-walls,
   That stand within the chace.

5 Beyond the lodge the city lies,
   Beneath its drift of smoke:
And ah! with what delighted eyes
   I turn to yonder oak.

In the poems of 1842, *The Talking Oak* first appeared. The
quotation from Mrs. Ritchie in the *Biographical Sketch*, concern-
ing the peculiarly English charm of Tennyson's writing applies,
perhaps, as forcibly to this poem as to anything in his work.
Remarkable, too, is the mastery displayed in combining accu-
rate botanical knowledge with poetic technic — two elements
that are
4. Chace

For when my passion first began,
10   Ere that, which in me burned,
The love, that makes me thrice a man,
    Could hope itself return'd ;

To yonder oak within the field
    I spoke without restraint,
15 And with a larger faith appeal'd
    Than Papist unto Saint.

For oft I talk'd with him apart,
    And told him of my choice,
Until he plagiarized a heart,
20   And answer'd with a voice.

Tho' what he whisper'd under Heaven
    None else could understand ;
I found him garrulously given,
    A babbler in the land.

25 But since I heard him make reply
    Is many a weary hour :
'T were well to question him, and try
    If yet he keeps the power.

Hail, hidden to the knees in fern,
30   Broad Oak of Sumner-chace,
Whose topmost branches can discern
    The roofs of Sumner-place !

Say thou, whereon I carved her name,
    If ever maid or spouse,
35 As fair as my Olivia, came

"O Walter, I have shelter'd here
   Whatever maiden grace
The good old Summers, year by year,
₄₀   Made ripe in Summer-chace:

"Old Summers, when the monk was fat,
   And, issuing shorn and sleek,
Would twist his girdle tight, and pat
   The girls upon the cheek,

₄₅ " Ere yet, in scorn of Peter's-pence,
   And number'd bead, and shrift,
Bluff Harry broke into the spence
   And turn'd the cowls adrift.

 " And I have seen some score of those
₅₀   Fresh faces, that would thrive
When his man-minded offset rose
   To chase the deer at five;

 " And all that from the town would stroll,
   Till that wild wind made work
₅₅ In which the gloomy brewer's soul
   Went by me, like a stork:

45–48 **Peter's-pence** was a tax to the Church of Rome, and
the whole stanza refers to the casting off of Papal authority by
Henry VIII, " Bluff Harry." The spence, line 47, was the
buttery or larder

51. His **man-minded offset.** Henry's daughter, Queen
Elizabeth

54 **That wild wind,** the storm which raged on the night of
Cromwell's death; it is said that his father was a brewer, and
tradition asserts that the stork, a Republican bird, disappeared
from England

"The slight she-slips of loyal blood,
 And others, passing praise,
Strait-laced, but all-too-full in bud
60 For puritanic stays:

 "And I have shadow'd many a group
 Of beauties, that were born
In teacup-times of hood and hoop,
 Or while the patch was worn;

55 "And, leg and arm with love-knots gay,
 About me leap'd and laugh'd
The modish Cupid of the day,
 And shrill'd his tinsel shaft.

 "I swear (and else may insects prick
70 Each leaf into a gall)
This girl, for whom your heart is sick,
 Is three times worth them all;

 "For those and theirs, by Nature's law,
 Have faded long ago;
75 But in these latter springs I saw
 Your own Olivia blow,

 "From when she gamboll'd on the greens
 A baby-germ, to when

57. **She-slips of loyal blood,** daughters of houses faithful
to the Stuarts. in the talk of an oak, they are naturally *slips*

63 **In teacup-times of hood and hoop**: this line and the
five that follow skillfully suggest the days of Queen Anne
and the artificialities of the eighteenth century

70. **Gall** = the lump that grows on the bark or leaves of a
tree round the eggs of an insect

U.

The maiden blossoms of her teens
_{so}   Could number five from ten.

" I swear, by leaf, and wind, and rain,
   (And hear me with thine ears,)
That, tho' I circle in the grain
   Five hundred rings of years —

35 " Yet, since I first could cast a shade,
   Did never creature pass
So slightly, musically made,
   So light upon the grass:

" For as to fairies, that will flit
30   To make the greensward fresh,
I hold them exquisitely knit,
   But far too spare of flesh."

Oh, hide thy knotted knees in fern,
   And overlook the chace;
45 And from thy topmost branch discern
   The roofs of Summer-place.

But thou, whereon I carved her name,
   That oft hast heard my vows,
Declare when last Olivia came
50   To sport beneath thy boughs.

" O yesterday, you know, the fair
   Was holden at the town;
Her father left his good arm-chair,
   And rode his hunter down.

U.

105 " And with him Albert came on his.
      I look'd at him with joy:
   As cowslip unto oxlip is,
      So seems she to the boy.

   " An hour had past — and, sitting straight
110   Within the low-wheel'd chaise,
   Her mother trundled to the gate
      Behind the dappled grays.

   " But, as for her, she stay'd at home,
      And on the roof she went,
115 And down the way you use to come
      She look'd with discontent.

   " She left the novel half-uncut
      Upon the rosewood shelf;
   She left the new piano shut:
120   She could not please herself.

   " Then ran she, gamesome as the colt,
      And livelier than a lark
   She sent her voice thro' all the holt
      Before her, and the park.

125 " A light wind chased her on the wing,
      And in the chase grew wild,
   As close as might be would he cling
      About the darling child:

   " But light as any wind that blows
0   So fleetly did she stir,
   The flower she touch'd on dipt and rose,

" And here she came, and round me play'd,
  And sang to me the whole
135 Of those three stanzas that you made
  About my ' giant bole ; '

" And in a fit of frolic mirth
  She strove to span my waist:
Alas, I was so broad of girth,
140 I could not be embraced.

" I wish'd myself the fair young beech
  That here beside me stands,
That round me, clasping each in each,
  She might have lock'd her hands.

145 " Yet seem'd the pressure thrice as sweet
  As woodbine's fragile hold,
Or when I feel about my feet
  The berried briony fold."

O muffle round thy knees with fern
150   And shadow Sumner-chace !
Long may thy topmost branch discern
  The roots of Sumner-place !

But tell me, did she read the name
  I carved with many vows
155 When last with throbbing heart I came
  To rest beneath thy boughs ?

" O yes, she wander'd round and round
  These knotted knees of mine,

And found, and kiss'd the name she found,
160   And sweetly murmur'd thine.

" A teardrop trembled from its source,
   And down my surface crept.
My sense of touch is something coarse,
   But I believe she wept.

165 " Then flush'd her cheek with rosy light,
   She glanced across the plain;
But not a creature was in sight:
   She kiss'd me once again.

" Her kisses were so close and kind,
170   That, trust me on my word,
Hard wood I am, and wrinkled rind,
   But yet my sap was stirr'd;

" And even into my inmost ring
   A pleasure I discern'd,
175 Like those blind motions of the Spring,
   That show the year is turn'd.

" Thrice-happy he that may caress
   The ringlet's waving balm —
The cushions of whose touch may press
180   The maiden's tender palm.

" I, rooted here among the groves,
   But languidly adjust
My vapid vegetable loves
   With anthers and with dust:

of this

185 " For ah! my friend, the days were brief
        Whereof the poets talk,
    When that, which breathes within the leaf,
        Could slip its bark and walk.

    " But could I, as in times foregone,
190   From spray, and branch, and stem,
    Have suck'd and gather'd into one
        The life that spreads in them,

    " She had not found me so remiss;
        But lightly issuing thro',
195 I would have paid her kiss for kiss,
        With usury thereto."

    O flourish high, with leafy towers,
        And overlook the lea,
    Pursue thy loves among the bowers
200   But leave thou mine to me.

    O flourish, hidden deep in fern,
        Old oak, I love thee well:
    A thousand thanks for what I learn
        And what remains to tell.

205 " 'T is little more: the day was warm;
        At last, tired out with play,
    She sank her head upon her arm
        And at my feet she lay.

    " Her eyelids dropp'd their silken eaves.
210   I breathed upon her eyes

" I took the swarming sound of life —
   The music from the town —
215 The murmurs of the drum and fife,
   And lull'd them in my own.

" Sometimes I let a sunbeam slip,
   To light her shaded eye ;
A second flutter'd round her lip
220   Like a golden butterfly ;

" A third would glimmer on her neck
   To make the necklace shine ;
Another slid, a sunny fleck,
   From head to ankle fine.

225 " Then close and dark my arms I spread,
   And shadow'd all her rest —
Dropt dews upon her golden head,
   An acorn in her breast.

" But in a pet she started up,
230   And pluck'd it out, and drew
My little oakling from the cup,
   And flung him in the dew.

" And yet it was a graceful gift —
   I felt a pang within
235 As when I see the woodman lift
   His axe to slay my kin.

" I shook him down because he was
   The finest on the tree.

"O kiss him twice and thrice for me,
　That have no lips to kiss,
For never yet was oak on lea
　Shall grow so fair as this."

245 Step deeper yet in herb and fern,
　Look further thro' the chace,
Spread upward till thy boughs discern
　The front of Sumner-place.

This fruit of thine by Love is blest,
250 　That but a moment lay
Where fairer fruit of Love may rest
　Some happy future day.

I kiss it twice, I kiss it thrice,
　The warmth it thence shall win
255 To riper life may magnetize
　The baby-oak within.

But thou, while kingdoms overset,
　Or lapse from hand to hand,
Thy leaf shall never fail, nor yet
260 　Thine acorn in the land.

May never saw dismember thee,
　Nor wielded axe disjoint,
That art the fairest-spoken tree
　From here to Lizard-point.

265 O rock upon thy towery top
　All throats that gurgle sweet!

264 **Li**　　　.
extremity

All starry culmination drop
  Balm-dews to bathe thy feet!

All grass of silky feather grow —
270   And while he sinks or swells
  The full south-breeze around thee blow
  The sound of minster bells.

The fat earth feed thy branchy root,
  That under deeply strikes!
275 The northern morning o'er thee shoot,
  High up, in silver spikes!

Nor ever lightning char thy grain,
  But, rolling as in sleep,
Low thunders bring the mellow rain,
280   That makes thee broad and deep!

And hear me swear a solemn oath,
  That only by thy side
Will I to Olive plight my troth,
  And gain her for my bride.

285 And when my marriage morn may fall,
  She, Dryad-like, shall wear
Alternate leaf and acorn-ball
  In wreath about her hair.

And I will work in prose and rhyme,
290   And praise thee more in both
Than bard has honor'd beech or lime,
  Or that Thessalian growth.

In which the swarthy ringdove sat,
   'And mystic sentence spoke;
295 And more than England honors that,
   Thy famous brother-oak,

Wherein the younger Charles abode
   Till all the paths were dim,
And far below the Roundhead rode,
300   And humm'd a surly hymn.

SEA DREAMS.

A city clerk, but gently born and bred;
His wife, an unknown artist's orphan child —
One babe was theirs, a Margaret, three years old:
They, thinking that her clear germander eye
5 Droopt in the giant-factoried city-gloom,
Came, with a month's leave given them, to the sea:
For which his gains were dock'd, however small:
Small were his gains, and hard his work; besides,
Their slender household fortunes (for the man
10 Had risk'd his little) like the little thrift,
Trembled in perilous places o'er a deep:
And oft, when sitting all alone, his face

which the oracles of Zeus were said to be delivered through
pigeons; another method was to interpret the rustling of the
leaves

295 **Thy famous brother-oak** the "Royal Oak" at
Boscobel in which Charles II hid after his defeat at Worcester
in 1651

Sea Dreams was produced in the same period with *I...*
... It was printed first in *Macmillan's Magazine*... Janu-
ary, 1860.
1 **City**

Would darken, as he cursed his credulousness,
And that one unctuous mouth which lured him, rogue,
15 To buy strange shares in some Peruvian mine.
Now seaward-bound for health they gain'd a coast,
All sand and cliff and deep-inrunning cave,
At close of day; slept, woke, and went the next,
The Sabbath, pious variers from the church,
20 To chapel; where a heated pulpiteer,
Not preaching simple Christ to simple men,
Announced the coming doom, and fulminated
Against the scarlet woman and her creed:
For sideways up he swung his arms, and shriek'd
25 "Thus, thus with violence," ev'n as if he held
The Apocalyptic millstone, and himself
Were that great Angel; "Thus with violence
Shall Babylon be cast into the sea;
Then comes the close." The gentle-hearted wife
30 Sat shuddering at the ruin of a world:
He at his own: but when the wordy storm
Had ended, forth they came and paced the shore,
Ran in and out the long sea-framing caves,
Drank the large air, and saw, but scarce believed
35 (The sootflake of so many a summer still
Clung to their fancies) that they saw, the sea.
So now on sand they walk'd, and now on cliff,
Lingering about the thymy promontories,
Till all the sails were darken'd in the west,

19. **Variers from the church.** Dissenters from the established church of England; their places of worship are called chapels, not churches.

23. **The scarlet woman** A favorite term with one class of "pulpiteers" for the Church of Rome

26 **The Apocalyptic millstone.** See Rev. xviii 21.

essary to

40 And rosëd in the east : then homeward and to bed :
Where she, who kept a tender Christian hope
Haunting a holy text, and still to that
Returning, as the bird returns, at night,
" Let not the sun go down upon your wrath,"
45 Said, " Love, forgive him : " but he did not speak :
And silenced by that silence lay the wife,
Remembering her dear Lord who died for all,
And musing on the little lives of men,
And how they mar this little by their feuds.

50   But while the two were sleeping, a full tide
Rose with ground-swell, which, on the foremost rocks
Touching, upjetted in spirts of wild sea-smoke,
And scaled in sheets of wasteful foam, and fell
In vast sea-cataracts — ever and anon
55 Dead claps of thunder from within the cliffs
Heard thro' the living roar. At this the babe,
Their Margaret cradled near them, wail'd and woke
The mother, and the father suddenly cried,
" A wreck, a wreck ! " then turn'd, and groaning said,

60   " Forgive ! How many will say, ' forgive,' and find
A sort of absolution in the sound
To hate a little longer ! No ; the sin
That neither God nor man can well forgive,
Hypocrisy, I saw it in him at once.
65 Is it so true that second thoughts are best ?
Not first, and third, which are a riper first ?
Too ripe, too late ! they come too late for use.
Ah love, there surely lives in man and beast
Something divine to warn them of their foes :

remember
and away

70 And such a sense, when first I fronted him,
Said, 'Trust him not;' but after, when I came
To know him more, I lost it, knew him less;
Fought with what seem'd my own uncharity;
Sat at his table; drank his costly wines;
75 Made more and more allowance for his talk;
Went further, fool! and trusted him with all,
All my poor scrapings from a dozen years
Of dust and deskwork: there is no such mine,
None: but a gulf of ruin, swallowing gold.
80 Not making. Ruin'd! ruin'd! the sea roars
Ruin: a fearful night!"

                "Not fearful; fair,"
Said the good wife, " if every star in heaven
Can make it fair: you do but hear the tide.
Had you ill dreams?"

              "O yes," he said, " I dream'd
85 Of such a tide swelling toward the land,
And I from out the boundless outer deep
Swept with it to the shore, and enter'd one
Of those dark caves that run beneath the cliffs.
I thought the motion of the boundless deep
90 Bore thro' the cave, and I was heaved upon it
In darkness: then I saw one lovely star
Larger and larger. 'What a world,' I thought,
'To live in!' but in moving on I found
Only the landward exit of the cave.
95 Bright with the sun upon the stream beyond;
And near the light a giant woman sat,
All over earthy, like a piece of earth,
A pickaxe in her hand: then out I slipt

100 As high as heaven, and every bird that sings:
And here the night-light flickering in my eyes
Awoke me."

" That was then your dream," she said,
" Not sad, but sweet."

" So sweet, I lay," said he,
" And mused upon it, drifting up the stream
105 In fancy, till I slept again, and pieced
The broken vision; for I dream'd that still
The motion of the great deep bore me on,
And that the woman walk'd upon the brink:
I wonder'd at her strength, and ask'd her of it:
110 ' It came,' she said, ' by working in the mines:'
O then to ask her of my shares, I thought:
And ask'd: but not a word: she shook her head.
And then the motion of the current ceased,
And there was rolling thunder; and we reach'd
115 A mountain, like a wall of burs and thorns:
But she with her strong feet up the steep hill
Trod out a path: I follow'd: and at top
She pointed seaward: there a fleet of glass,
That seem'd a fleet of jewels under me,
120 Sailing along before a gloomy cloud
That not one moment ceased to thunder, past
In sunshine: right across its track there lay,
Down in the water, a long reef of gold,
Or what seem'd gold: and I was glad at first
125 To think that in our often-ransack'd world
Still so much gold was left: and then I fear'd
Lest the gay navy there should splinter on it
And
An

130 (I thought I could have died to save it) near'd,
Touch'd, clink'd, and clash'd, and vanish'd, and I
woke.
I heard the clash so clearly. Now I see
My dream was Life ; the woman honest Work ;
And my poor venture but a fleet of glass
135 Wreck'd on a reef of visionary gold."

" Nay," said the kindly wife to comfort him,
" You raised your arm, you tumbled down and broke
The glass with little Margaret's medicine in it ;
And, breaking that, you made and broke your dream :
140 A trifle makes a dream, a trifle breaks."

" No trifle," groan'd the husband ; " yesterday
I met him suddenly in the street, and ask'd
That which I ask'd the woman in my dream.
Like her he shook his head. ' Show me the books ! '
145 He dodged me with a long and loose account.
' The books, the books ! ' but he, he could not wait,
Bound on a matter he of life and death :
When the great Books (see Daniel seven and ten)
Were open'd, I should find he meant me well ;
150 And then began to bloat himself, and ooze
All over with the fat affectionate smile
That makes the widow lean. ' My dearest friend,
Have faith, have faith ! We live by faith,' said he
' And all things work together for the good

148. " The judgment was set, and the books were opened "
Dan. vii 10   As in *Enoch Arden* the character of Annie is
kept consistent by her superstitions, so here the familiar use
of the Scriptures by the city clerk and his wife mark them as
" pious varners from the church " (line 19).

that love

155 Of those ' — it makes me sick to quote him — last
Gript my hand hard, and with God-bless-you went.
I stood like one that had received a blow :
I found a hard friend in his loose accounts,
A loose one in the hard grip of his hand,
160 A curse in his God-bless-you : then my eyes
Pursued him down the street, and far away,
Among the honest shoulders of the crowd,
Read rascal in the motions of his back,
And scoundrel in the supple-sliding knee."

165   " Was he so bound, poor soul ? " said the good
       wife ;
" So are we all : but do not call him, love,
Before you prove him, rogue, and proved, forgive.
His gain is loss : for he that wrongs his friend
Wrongs himself more, and ever bears about
170 A silent court of justice in his breast,
Himself the judge and jury, and himself
The prisoner at the bar, ever condemn'd :
And that drags down his life : then comes what
       comes
Hereafter : and he meant, he said he meant,
175 Perhaps he meant, or partly meant, you well.'

     " ' With all his conscience and one eye askew ' —
Love, let me quote these lines, that you may learn
A man is likewise counsel for himself,
Too often, in that silent court of yours —
180 ' With all his conscience and one eye askew,
So false, he partly took himself for true :
Whose pious talk, when most his heart was dry,

Made wet the crafty crowsfoot round his eye;
Who, never naming God except for gain,
185 So never took that useful name in vain;
Made Him his catspaw and the Cross his tool,
And Christ the bait to trap his dupe and fool;
Nor deeds of gift, but gifts of grace he forged,
And snakelike slimed his victim ere he gorged;
190 And oft at Bible meetings, o'er the rest
Arising, did his holy oily best,
Dropping the too rough H in Hell and Heaven,
To spread the Word by which himself had thriven.'
How like you this old satire?"

                    " Nay," she said,
195 " I loathe it: he had never kindly heart,
Nor ever cared to better his own kind,
Who first wrote satire, with no pity in it.
But will you hear *my* dream, for I had one
That altogether went to music?   Still
200 It awed me."

             Then she told it, having dream'd
Of that same coast.

             — " But round the North, a light,
A belt, it seem'd, of luminous vapor, lay,
And ever in it a low musical note
Swell'd up and died; and, as it swell'd, a ridge
205 Of breaker issued from the belt, and still
Grew with the growing note, and when the note
Had reach'd a thunderous fullness, on those cliffs
Broke, mixt with awful light (the same as that

Living within the belt) whereby she saw
110 That all those lines of cliffs were cliffs no more,
But huge cathedral fronts of every age,
Grave, florid, stern, as far as eye could see,
One after one : and then the great ridge drew,
Lessening to the lessening music, back,
215 And past into the belt and swell'd again
Slowly to music : ever when it broke
The statues, king or saint, or founder, fell :
Then from the gaps and chasms of ruin left
Came men and women in dark clusters round,
220 Some crying 'Set them up! they shall not fall!'
And others 'Let them lie, for they have fall'n.'
And still they strove and wrangled : and she grieved
In her strange dream, she knew not why, to find
Their wildest wailings never out of tune
225 With that sweet note : and ever as their shrieks
Ran highest up the gamut, that great wave
Returning, while none mark'd it, on the crowd
Broke, mixt with awful light, and show'd their eyes
Glaring, and passionate looks, and swept away
230 The men of flesh and blood, and men of stone,
To the waste deeps together.

                              "Then I fixt
My wistful eyes on two fair images,
Both crown'd with stars and high among the stars,
The Virgin Mother standing with her child
235 High up on one of those dark minster-fronts—

is so clear as to need no explanation, and once the vision is to
show, lines 230-241 that dreams after all signify nothing, it is
not more reasonable to take her stars merely for what they chance
to be on
than those

Till she began to totter, and the child
Clung to the mother, and sent out a cry
Which mixt with little Margaret's, and I woke,
And my dream awed me : — well — but what are
     dreams !
240 Yours came but from the breaking of a glass,
And mine but from the crying of a child."

  "Child? No!" said he, " but this tide's roar,
     and his.
Our Boanerges with his threats of doom,
And loud-lung'd Antibabylonianisms
245 (Altho' I grant but little music there)
Went both to make your dream : but if there
     were
A music harmonizing our wild cries,
Sphere-music such as that you dream'd about,
Why, that would make our passions far too like
250 The discords dear to the musician. No —
One shriek of hate would jar all the hymns of
     heaven :
True Devils with no ear, they howl in tune
With nothing but the Devil!"

                              " 'True' indeed!
One of our town, but later by an hour
255 Here than ourselves, spoke with me on the shore ;
While you were running down the sands, and
     made
The dimpled flounce of the sea-furbelow flap,

243. **Boanerges** See line 20. " And he surnamed them
Boanerges, which is, the sons of thunder." St Mark iii. 17
257. **The sea-furbelow** : an unfamiliar name for a large
                              . ed flounce.

Good man, to please the child. She brought strange
    news.
Why were you silent when I spoke to-night?
250 I had set my heart on your forgiving him
Before you knew. We *must* forgive the dead."

"Dead! who is dead?"

"The man your eye pursued.
A little after you had parted with him,
He suddenly dropt dead of heart-disease."

260 "Dead? he? of heart-disease? what heart had he
To die of? Dead!"

"Ah, dearest, if there be
A devil in man, there is an angel too,
And if he did that wrong you charge him with,
His angel broke his heart. But your rough voice
270 (You spoke so loud) has roused the child again.
Sleep, little birdie, sleep! will she not sleep
Without her 'little birdie'? well then, sleep,
And I will sing you 'birdie.'"

Saying this,
The woman half turn'd round from him she
    loved,
280 Left him one hand, and reaching thro' the night
Her other, found (for it was close beside)
And half embraced the basket cradle-head
With one soft arm, which, like the pliant bough

like edge
in Rolfe's

That moving moves the nest and nestling, sway'd
280 The cradle, while she sang this baby song.

> What does little birdie say
> In her nest at peep of day ?
> Let me fly, says little birdie,
> Mother, let me fly away.
> 285 Birdie, rest a little longer,
> Till the little wings are stronger.
> So she rests a little longer,
> Then she flies away.
>
> What does little baby say,
> 290 In her bed at peep of day ?
> Baby says, like little birdie,
> Let me rise and fly away.
> Baby, sleep a little longer,
> Till the little limbs are stronger.
> 295 If she sleeps a little longer,
> Baby too shall fly away.

" She sleeps : let us too, let all evil, sleep.
He also sleeps — another sleep than ours.
He can do no more wrong : forgive him, dear,
300 And I shall sleep the sounder ! "

                              Then the man,
" His deeds yet live, the worst is yet to come.
Yet let your sleep for this one night be sound :
I do forgive him ! "

                    " Thanks, my love," she said,
" Your own will be the sweeter," and they slept.

U.

ODE ON THE DEATH OF THE DUKE OF WELLINGTON.

I.

Bury the Great Duke
  With an empire's lamentation.
Let us bury the Great Duke
  To the noise of the mourning of a mighty nation.
Mourning when their leaders fall,
Warriors carry the warrior's pall,
And sorrow darkens hamlet and hall.

II.

Where shall we lay the man whom we deplore?
Here, in streaming London's central roar.
Let the sound of those he wrought for,
And the feet of those he fought for,
Echo round his bones for evermore.

Arthur Wellesley, Duke of Wellington, died September 12, 185_. The first draft of the *Ode* was hastily written, and published as a sixteen-page pamphlet. In this form it received severe criticism, but when it appeared again a year later, it was much emended. Besides minor alterations lines were added to stanzas i. and ii. and the passage about Lisbon in the sixth stanza was included.

Different as Wellington was from Lincoln in many outward ways, it is interesting to observe how many lines which the Laureate wrote of the one might have been written of the other. It is somewhat less strange that the high patriotism celebrated in stanzas vii. and viii. appeals to citizens of every land.

9. In streaming London's central roar. St. Paul's Cathedral *U.*

III.

Lead out the pageant: sad and slow,
 As fits an universal woe,
15 Let the long, long procession go,
And let the sorrowing crowd about it grow,
And let the mournful martial music blow;
The last great Englishman is low.

IV.

Mourn, for to us he seems the last,
20 Remembering all his greatness in the Past.
No more in soldier fashion will he greet
With lifted hand the gazer in the street.
O friends, our chief state-oracle is mute:
Mourn for the man of long-enduring blood,
25 The statesman-warrior, moderate, resolute,
Whole in himself, a common good.
Mourn for the man of amplest influence,
Yet clearest of ambitious crime.
Our greatest yet with least pretence,
30 Great in council and great in war,
Foremost captain of his time,
Rich in saving common-sense,
And, as the greatest only are,
In his simplicity sublime.
35 O good gray head which all men knew,
O voice from which their omens all men drew,
O iron nerve to true occasion true,
O fall'n at length that tower of strength

18. The last great Englishman is low. Compare this
'ine and the stanza iv. following with Lowell's *Commemoration*
 as "the

Which stood four-square to all the winds that blew!
40 Such was he whom we deplore.
   The long self-sacrifice of life is o'er.
   The great World-victor's victor will be seen no more.

v.

   All is over and done:
   Render thanks to the Giver,
45 England, for thy son.
   Let the bell be toll'd.
   Render thanks to the Giver,
   And render him to the mould.
   Under the cross of gold
50 That shines over city and river,
   There he shall rest for ever
   Among the wise and the bold.
   Let the bell be toll'd:
   And a reverent people behold
55 The towering car, the sable steeds:
   Bright let it be with its blazon'd deeds,
   Dark in its funeral fold.
   Let the bell be toll'd:
   And a deeper knell in the heart be knoll'd;
60 And the sound of the sorrowing anthem roll'd
   Thro' the dome of the golden cross;
   And the volleying cannon thunder his loss;
   He knew their voices of old.
   For many a time in many a clime

42. The great **World-victor** = Napoleon
46. **Let the bell be toll'd**: it may be noticed how the repetition of this line and the sound in the passage that follows, of the rhymes with *toll'd*, produce the effect of solemnity that is sought. *U*

65 His captain's-ear has heard them boom
Bellowing victory, bellowing doom :
When he with those deep voices wrought,
Guarding realms and kings from shame ;
With those deep voices our dead captain taught
70 The tyrant, and asserts his claim
In that dread sound to the great name,
Which he has worn so pure of blame,
In praise and in dispraise the same,
A man of well-attemper'd frame.
75 O civic muse, to such a name,
To such a name for ages long,
To such a name,
Preserve a broad approach of fame,
And ever-echoing avenues of song.

VI.

80 Who is he that cometh, like an honor'd guest,
With banner and with music, with soldier and with
priest,
With a nation weeping, and breaking on my rest ?
Mighty Seaman, this is he
Was great by land as thou by sea.
85 Thine island loves thee well, thou famous man,
The greatest sailor since our world began.
Now, to the roll of muffled drums,
To thee the greatest soldier comes :
For this is he
90 Was great by land as thou by sea ;
His foes were thine : he kept us free ;
O give him welcome, this is he
Worthy of our gorgeous rites,

90 Mighty Seaman . . . . d in St.
P4

And worthy to be laid by thee;
95 For this is England's greatest son,
He that gain'd a hundred fights,
Nor ever lost an English gun;
This is he that far away
Against the myriads of Assaye
100 Clash'd with his fiery few and won;
And underneath another sun,
Warring on a later day,
Round affrighted Lisbon drew
The treble works, the vast designs
105 Of his labor'd rampart-lines,
Where he greatly stood at bay,
Whence he issued forth anew,
And ever great and greater grew,
Beating from the wasted vines
110 Back to France her banded swarms,
Back to France with countless blows,
Till o'er the hills her eagles flew
Beyond the Pyrenean pines,
Follow'd up in valley and glen
115 With blare of bugle, clamor of men,
Roll of cannon and clash of arms,
And England pouring on her foes,
Such a war had such a close.
Again their ravening eagle rose
120 In anger, wheel'd on Europe-shadowing wings,
And barking for the thrones of kings;
Till one that sought but Duty's iron crown

99 **Assaye** Wellington's first great battle, in India, September 23, 1803. With 9,600 men he defeated 10,000.

103 **Affrighted Lisbon** in the battle of Vimeira, August 21,
1808, the
base of the

On that loud sabbath shook the spoiler down;
A day of onsets of despair!
125 Dash'd on every rocky square
Their surging charges foam'd themselves away;
Last, the Prussian trumpet blew;
Thro' the long-tormented air
Heaven flash'd a sudden jubilant ray,
130 And down we swept and charged and overthrew.
So great a soldier taught us there,
What long-enduring hearts could do
In that world-earthquake, Waterloo!
Mighty Seaman, tender and true,
135 And pure as he from taint of craven guile,
O saviour of the silver-coasted isle,
O shaker of the Baltic and the Nile,
If aught of things that here befall
Touch a spirit among things divine,
140 If love of country move thee there at all,
Be glad, because his bones are laid by thine!
And thro' the centuries let a people's voice
In full acclaim,
A people's voice,
145 The proof and echo of all human fame,
A people's voice, when they rejoice
At civic revel and pomp and game,
Attest their great commander's claim
With honor, honor, honor, honor to him,
150 Eternal honor to his name.

123. **That loud sabbath**, the day of the battle of Waterloo.

138 **O shaker of the Baltic and the Nile**, in the battle
of the Baltic, Nelson, with Admiral Parker, defeated the Danish
fle ___ ___ ___ ___ ___ ___ ___ Nile he
w

VII.

A people's voice! we are a people yet.
Tho' all men else their nobler dreams forget,
Confus'd by brainless mobs and lawless Powers;
Thank Him who isled us here, and roughly set
155 His Briton in blown seas and storming showers,
We have a voice, with which to pay the debt
Of boundless love and reverence and regret
To those great men who fought, and kept it ours.
And keep it ours, O God, from brute control;
160 O Statesmen, guard us, guard the eye, the soul
Of Europe, keep our noble England whole,
And save the one true seed of freedom sown
Betwixt a people and their ancient throne,
That sober freedom out of which there springs
165 Our loyal passion for our temperate kings;
For, saving that, ye help to save mankind
Till public wrong be crumbled into dust,
And drill the raw world for the march of mind,
Till crowds at length be sane and crowns be just.
170 But wink no more in slothful overtrust.
Remember him who led your hosts;
He bade you guard the sacred coasts.
Your cannons moulder on the seaward wall;
His voice is silent in your council-hall
175 For ever; and whatever tempests lour
For ever silent: even if they broke
In thunder, silent; yet remember all
He spoke among you, and the Man who spoke;
Who never sold the truth to serve the hour,
180 Nor palter'd with Eternal God for power.

168 D
the world
170 W....   ...

Who let the turbid streams of rumor flow
Thro' either babbling world of high and low ;
Whose life was work. whose language rife
With rugged maxims hewn from life ;
185 Who never spoke against a foe ;
Whose eighty winters freeze with one rebuke
All great self-seekers trampling on the right :
Truth-teller was our England's Alfred named ;
Truth-lover was our English Duke ;
190 Whatever record leap to light
He never shall be shamed.

VIII.

Lo. the leader in these glorious wars
Now to glorious burial slowly borne,
Follow'd by the brave of other lands,
195 He, on whom from both her open hands
Lavish Honor shower'd all her stars,
And affluent Fortune emptied all her horn.
Yea, let all good things await
Him who cares not to be great.
200 But as he saves or serves the state.
Not once or twice in our rough island-story,
The path of duty was the way to glory :
He that walks it, only thirsting
For the right, and learns to deaden
205 Love of self. before his journey closes.
He shall find the stubborn thistle bursting
Into glossy purples. which outredden
All voluptuous garden-roses.
Not once or twice in our fair i-land-story,
210 The path of duty was the way to glory :

181 Rugged maxims hewn from life, another line that

He, that ever following her commands,
On with toil of heart and knees and hands,
Thro' the long gorge to the far light has won
His path upward, and prevail'd.
21 Shall find the toppling crags of Duty scaled
Are close upon the shining table-lands
To which our God Himself is moon and sun.
Such was he, his work is done.
But while the races of mankind endure,
220 Let his great example stand
Colossal, seen of every land,
And keep the soldier firm, the statesman pure:
Till in all lands and thro' all human story
The path of duty be the way to glory:
225 And let the land whose hearths he saved from shame
For many and many an age proclaim
At civic revel and pomp and game,
And when the long-illumined cities flame
Their ever-loyal iron leader's fame,
230 With honor, honor, honor, honor to him,
Eternal honor to his name.

IX.

Peace, his triumph will be sung
By some yet unmoulded tongue
Far on in summers that we shall not see:
235 Peace, it is a day of pain
For one about whose patriarchal knee
Late the little children clung:
O peace, it is a day of pain
For one, upon whose hand and heart and brain
24 Once the weight and fate of Europe hung.

Ours the pain, be his the gain!
More than is of man's degree
Must be with us, watching here
At this, our great solemnity.
245 Whom we see not we revere;
We revere, and we refrain
From talk of battles loud and vain,
And brawling memories all too free
For such a wise humility
250 As befits a solemn fane:
We revere, and while we hear
The tides of Music's golden sea
Setting toward eternity,
Uplifted high in heart and hope are we,
255 Until we doubt not that for one so true
There must be other nobler work to do
Than when he fought at Waterloo,
And Victor he must ever be.
For tho' the Giant Ages heave the hill
260 And break the shore, and evermore
Make and break, and work their will;
Tho' world on world in myriad myriads roll
Round us, each with different powers,
And other forms of life than ours,
265 What know we greater than the soul?
On God and Godlike men we build our trust.
Hush, the Dead March wails in the people's ears:
The dark crowd moves, and there are sobs and tears·
The black earth yawns: the mortal disappears;
270 Ashes to ashes, dust to dust;
He is gone who seem'd so great. —
Gone: but nothing can bereave him
Of the force he made his own

U

225 Something far advanced in State,
And that he wears a truer crown
Than any wreath that man can weave him.
Speak no more of his renown,
Lay your earthly fancies down,
230 And in the vast cathedral leave him.
God accept him, Christ receive him.

ULYSSES.

It little profits that an idle king,
By this still hearth, among these barren crags,
Match'd with an aged wife, I meet and dole
Unequal laws unto a savage race.
5 That hoard, and sleep, and feed, and know not me.
I cannot rest from travel: I will drink
Life to the lees: all times I have enjoy'd
Greatly, have suffer'd greatly, both with those
That loved me, and alone; on shore, and when
10 Thro' scudding drifts the rainy Hyades
Vext the dim sea: I am become a name;
For always roaming with a hungry heart
Much have I seen and known: cities of men
And manners, climates, councils, governments,

Ulysses appeared first in the volume of 1842. An interesting circumstance in connection with it is that when Sir Robert Peel as Prime Minister was urged to put Tennyson's name on the pension list in 1845, he confessed complete ignorance of the poet's work. The reading of this one poem, however, decided him to grant the annuity.

10 **Hyades** = "the rainers," the group of seven stars at the head of Taurus.

11 **U.** word

15 Myself not least, but honor'd of them all;
And drunk delight of battle with my peers,
Far on the ringing plains of windy Troy.
I am a part of all that I have met;
Yet all experience is an arch wherethro'
20 Gleams that untravell'd world, whose margin fades
For ever and for ever when I move.
How dull it is to pause, to make an end,
To rust unburnish'd, not to shine in use!
As tho' to breathe were life. Life piled on life
25 Were all too little, and of one to me
Little remains; but every hour is saved
From that eternal silence, something more,
A bringer of new things; and vile it were
For some three suns to store and hoard myself,
30 And this gray spirit yearning in desire
To follow knowledge like a sinking star,
Beyond the utmost bound of human thought.
This is my son, mine own Telemachus,
To whom I leave the sceptre and the isle —
35 Well-loved of me, discerning to fulfil
This labor, by slow prudence to make mild
A rugged people, and thro' soft degrees
Subdue them to the useful and the good.
Most blameless is he, centred in the sphere
40 Of common duties, decent not to fail
In offices of tenderness, and pay
Meet adoration to my household gods,
When I am gone. He works his work, I mine
There lies the port: the vessel puffs her sail:
45 There gloom the dark broad seas. My mariners,
Souls that have toil'd, and wrought, and thought
with me —

The thunder and the sunshine, and opposed
Free hearts, free foreheads—you and I are old;
50 Old age hath yet his honor and his toil;
Death closes all: but something ere the end,
Some work of noble note may yet be done,
Not unbecoming men that strove with Gods.
The lights begin to twinkle from the rocks:
55 The long day wanes: the slow moon climbs: the
    deep
Moans round with many voices. Come, my friends,
'T is not too late to seek a newer world.
Push off, and sitting well in order smite
The sounding furrows; for my purpose holds
60 To sail beyond the sunset, and the baths
Of all the western stars, until I die.
It may be that the gulfs will wash us down:
It may be we shall touch the Happy Isles.
And see the great Achilles, whom we knew.
65 Tho' much is taken, much abides; and tho'
We are not now that strength which in old days
Moved earth and heaven; that which we are, we
    are:
One equal temper of heroic hearts,
Made weak by time and fate, but strong in will
70 To strive, to seek, to find, and not to yield.

60. **The baths, etc** Where the western stars sink into the
sea.

U.

THE CHARGE OF THE LIGHT BRIGADE.

I.

HALF a league, half a league,
Half a league onward,
All in the valley of Death
    Rode the six hundred.
5 "Forward the Light Brigade!
Charge for the guns!" he said:
Into the valley of Death
    Rode the six hundred.

II.

"Forward the Light Brigade!"
10 Was there a man dismay'd?
Not tho' the soldier knew

The Charge of the Light Brigade was first printed in a London daily newspaper in December, 1854, with a note by the author saying it was prompted by his "reading the first report of the *Times'* correspondent, where only six hundred and seven sabres are mentioned as having taken part in the charge." Balaklava, where the charge took place, was the British headquarters, in the Crimean War, from September, 1854 to June, 1856; the charge itself was made October 25, 1854. From the military point of view it was an absurd and hopeless movement. The order which occasioned it was a blunder. Captain Nolan, on whom it fell to deliver the command, was the first man to fall.

In the volume of 1855, the poem appeared considerably amended, but the changes were so criticised that the poet restored the lines more nearly to their original form. Moreover, he had a thousand copies of them printed in leaflets for distribution among the soldiers before Sebastopol; for he had heard how they liked the poem, and wanted them, as he said in a note
written to them "to know that the men that fought at home love and

Some one had blunder'd:
Theirs not to make reply
Theirs not to reason why,
15 Theirs but to do and die:
Into the valley of Death
Rode the six hundred.

III.

Cannon to right of them,
Cannon to left of them,
20 Cannon in front of them
Volley'd and thunder'd:
Storm'd at with shot and shell,
Boldly they rode and well,
Into the jaws of Death,
25 Into the mouth of Hell
Rode the six hundred.

IV.

Flash'd all their sabres bare,
Flash'd as they turn'd in air
Sabring the gunners there,
30 Charging an army, while
All the world wonder'd:
Plunged in the battery-smoke
Right thro' the line they broke;
Cossack and Russian
35 Reel'd from the sabre-stroke
Shatter'd and sunder'd.
Then they rode back, but not
Not the six hundred.

U

40 Cannon to left of them.

Cannon behind them
　　Volley'd and thunder'd ;
Storm'd at with shot and shell,
While horse and hero fell,
45 They that had fought so well
Came thro' the jaws of Death
Back from the mouth of Hell,
All that was left of them,
　　Left of six hundred.

VI.

50 When can their glory fade ?
　O the wild charge they made !
　　All the world wonder'd.
Honor the charge they made !
Honor the Light Brigade,
55　Noble six hundred !

LADY CLARE.

It was the time when lilies blow,
　And clouds are highest up in air,
Lord Ronald brought a lily-white doe
　To give his cousin, Lady Clare.

5 I trow they did not part in scorn :
　Lovers long-betroth'd were they :
They two will wed the morrow morn :
　God's blessing on the day !

Lady Clare appeared in the volume of 1842. and there the poet
acknowledged in a note his debt to Miss Ferrier's novel *The In-
heritance* for the story. As the substance of the verses is like
tha ᵉ   irkable
dé

"He does not love me for my birth,
10 Nor for my lands so broad and fair;
He loves me for my own true worth,
    And that is well," said Lady Clare.

In there came old Alice the nurse,
    Said, "Who was this that went from thee?"
15 "It was my cousin," said Lady Clare,
    "To-morrow he weds with me."

"O God be thank'd!" said Alice the nurse,
    "That all comes round so just and fair:
Lord Ronald is heir of all your lands,
20   And you are *not* the Lady Clare."

"Are ye out of your mind, my nurse, my nurse?"
    Said Lady Clare, "that ye speak so wild?"
"As God's above," said Alice the nurse,
    "I speak the truth: you are my child.

25 "The old Earl's daughter died at my breast;
    I speak the truth, as I live by bread!
I buried her like my own sweet child,
    And put my child in her stead."

"Falsely, falsely have ye done,
30   O mother," she said, "if this be true,
To keep the best man under the sun
    So many years from his due."

"Nay now, my child," said Alice the nurse,
    "But keep the secret for your life,
35 And ﹒" ᵎ   ⸱⸱⸱ ⸱ ⸱ ⸱ ᵎ ᵎ
    Wi﹒   ⸱   ⸱ ⸱ ⸱

" If I 'm a beggar born," she said,
  " I will speak out, for I dare not lie.
Pull off, pull off, the brooch of gold,
40   And fling the diamond necklace by."

  " Nay now, my child," said Alice the nurse,
    " But keep the secret all ye can."
She said, " Not so: but I will know
  If there be any faith in man."

45 " Nay now, what faith? " said Alice the nurse,
    " The man will cleave unto his right."
  " And he shall have it," the lady replied,
    " Tho' I should die to-night."

  " Yet give one kiss to your mother dear !
50   Alas, my child, I sinn'd for thee."
  " O mother, mother, mother," she said,
    " So strange it seems to me.

  " Yet here 's a kiss for my mother dear,
    My mother dear, if this be so,
55 And lay your hand upon my head,
    And bless me, mother, ere I go."

  She clad herself in a russet gown,
    She was no longer Lady Clare:
She went by dale, and she went by down,
60   With a single rose in her hair.

  The lily-white doe Lord Ronald had brought
    Leapt up from where she lay,
Dropt her head in the maiden's hand.

65 Down stept Lord Ronald from his tower:
  " O Lady Clare, you shame your worth!
Why come you drest like a village maid,
  That are the flower of the earth? "

  " If I come drest like a village maid,
70   I am but as my fortunes are:
I am a beggar born," she said,
    " And not the Lady Clare."

  "Play me no tricks," said Lord Ronald,
  " For I am yours in word and in deed.
75 Play me no tricks," said Lord Ronald,
  " Your riddle is hard to read."

  O and proudly stood she up!
    Her heart within her did not fail;
She look'd into Lord Ronald's eyes,
80   And told him all her nurse's tale.

  He laugh'd a laugh of merry scorn:
    He turn'd and kiss'd her where she stood:
" If you are not the heiress born,
    And I," said he, " the next in blood —

85 " If you are not the heiress born,
    And I," said he, " the lawful heir,
We two will wed to-morrow morn,
    And you shall still be Lady Clare."

  73 **Lord Ronald'**; the necessity of accenting Ronald here,
on the second syllable, is one of the marks of the ballad stru*
ture
  77 O...

THE DEATH OF THE OLD YEAR.

FULL knee-deep lies the winter snow,
And the winter winds are wearily sighing.
Toll ye the church-bell sad and slow,
And tread softly and speak low,
5 For the old year lies a-dying.
  Old year, you must not die;
  You came to us so readily,
  You lived with us so steadily,
  Old year, you shall not die.

10 He lieth still : he doth not move :
He will not see the dawn of day.
He hath no other life above.
He gave me a friend, and a true true-love,
And the New-year will take 'em away.
15 Old year, you must not go ;
  So long as you have been with us,
  Such joy as you have seen with us,
  Old year, you shall not go.

He froth'd his bumpers to the brim ;
20 A jollier year we shall not see.
But tho' his eyes are waxing dim,
And tho' his foes speak ill of him,
He was a friend to me.
  Old year, you shall not die ;
25 We did so laugh and cry with you,
  I 've half a mind to die with you,
  Old year, if you must die.

The Death of the Old Year first appeared in the volume of
18..

He was full of joke and jest,
But all his merry quips are o'er.
30 To see him die, across the waste
His son and heir doth ride post-haste,
But he 'll be dead before.
  Every one for his own.
  The night is starry and cold, my friend,
35 And the New-year blithe and bold, my friend,
  Comes up to take his own.

How hard he breathes! over the snow
I heard just now the crowing cock.
The shadows flicker to and fro:
40 The cricket chirps: the light burns low:
'T is nearly twelve o'clock.
  Shake hands, before you die.
  Old year, we 'll dearly rue for you:
  What is it we can do for you?
45 Speak out before you die.

His face is growing sharp and thin.
Alack! our friend is gone.
Close up his eyes: tie up his chin:
Step from the corpse, and let him in
50 That standeth there alone,
  And waiteth at the door.
  There 's a new foot on the floor, my friend,
  And a new face at the door, my friend,
  A new face at the door.

U.

Lightning Source UK Ltd.
Milton Keynes UK
UKHW021847060921
390144UK00002B/204